Establishing a System of

Policies and

Procedures

Establishing a System of Policies and Procedures

Setting Up a Successful
Policies and Procedures System
for Printed, On-line, and
Web Manuals

Stephen B. Page
MBA, PMP, CSQE, CRM, CFC

Process Improvement Publishing
spage@columbus.rr.com

Address Printing questions to:

Steve Page
PO BOX 1694
Westerville, Ohio 43086, USA
Email: spage@columbus.rr.com
VOICE: (614) 323-3617
FAX: Send email for current fax number

Ordering Information

Individual Sales: This book may be ordered through the author's web site at http://www.companymanuals.com/index.htm or through the above address.

Orders by U.S. trade bookstores and wholesalers: Please contact the author at the above address for pricing and shipping terms.

Page, Stephen B. (1949 -)
    Establishing a System of Policies and Procedures: Setting up a Successful Policies and Procedures System, Printed, Online, and Web Manuals. Includes references and appendices.
    ISBN: 1-929065-00-0

Published June 21, 1998   Reprinted May 15, 1999
Revised August 4, 2000   Reprinted September 1, 2001
Revised November 1, 2000   Revised November 15, 2002
Reprinted March 12, 2005

ACKNOWLEDGMENTS

Thanks go to all my friends and previous companies where I have worked for allowing me to implement the policies and procedures system outlined in this book. The system has proved to be very successful since the market is almost void of practical books on policies and procedures. I have taken the initiative and have written this book to outline my successes.

This book has been well received by those readers who want a simple and yet effective book for writing a system of policies and procedures. I have found that most companies try to publish their policies and procedures manuals in a variety of formats including print, online, web, CD-ROM, and video media. I wish to thank my past and current employers for giving me the opportunity to test my theories and provide practical feedback on the delivered products, the intent of which is to assure that one is getting a method of developing a system of policies and procedures that are representative of the best practices of developing policies and procedures in the industry.

I wish to thank Joseph Burrow for editing this book. He is currently the Academic Director of a small English school, a Second Language School located in Washington, D.C. A graduate of New York University's Tisch School of the Arts, Mr. Burrow recently returned from Italy where he had been pursuing a career in Opera Performance.

I sincerely thank my wife for allowing me the time to spend countless hours on researching, writing, rewriting, editing, and promoting this subject matter. She has been very understanding and supportive of my efforts.

This book is dedicated to all individuals who have been assigned or who have taken on the task to establish, revise, or re-engineer a policies and procedures system.

Books by Stephen B. Page
(Reading Sequence)

Book Title	Website
Establishing a System of Policies and Procedures, ISBN: 1929065000. Copyright 1998, 2002, 168 Pages	*http://www.companymanuals.com/ index.htm*
7 Steps to Better Written Policies and Procedures, ISBN: 1929065248. Copyright 2001, 126 Pages	*http://www.companymanuals.com/ writingformat/index.htm*
Best Practices in Policies and Procedures, ISBN: 1929065078. Copyright 2002, 168 Pages	*http://www.companymanuals.com/ bestpractices/index.htm*
Achieving 100% Compliance of Policies and Procedures, ISBN: 1929065493. Copyright 2000, 359 Pages	*http://www.companymanuals.com/ compliance/index.htm*

HOW TO CONTACT THIS AUTHOR

Stephen B. Page is interested in helping others. He will answer questions about business processes, policies, and procedures as a free service. He can be reached in any of the following ways:

Stephen B. Page
PO BOX 1694
Westerville, Ohio 43086
Email: spage@columbus.rr.com
VOICE: (614) 323-3617
FAX: Send email for most current fax number
URL: http://www.companymanuals.com/index.htm

TABLE OF CONTENTS

About the Author
Preface
Introduction

CHAPTER 1 1

The Need for Policies and Procedures

- Strategic Role of Policies and Procedures
- Business Processes
- Visions
- Policy and Procedure Definitions
- Internal Control System
- Organizational Structure for Policies and Procedures
- Eight Reasons for Documenting Policies and Procedures
- Managing the Policies and Procedures Function
- Six Decisions for the Policies and Procedures Department
- Company Manuals
- Hiring Decisions

CHAPTER 2 17

Research Methods

- Importance of Research to a Policies and Procedures System
- Target of Research
- Determining Content for Manuals
- Business Process Reengineering
- Reviewing Core Business Processes
- Benchmarking
- Networking
- Coordinating Ideas with Forms Management
- External Sources that Influence Content: ISO 9000 Series and Capability Maturity Model
- Determining the Details behind Policies and Procedures
- Cross-Functional Teams
- Conducting Meetings and Selecting Meeting Topics
- Selection of Alternate Solutions

- Developing the Selected Alternate Solution
- Brainstorming Ideas
- Conversion of Selected Alternate to Writing Format
- Special Skills Required: Speaking and Listening
- Note Taking
- Flow Charts

CHAPTER 3 37

Forms Management

- Vital Importance of Forms Control
- Forms and Procedures Analysts Working Together
- Forms Explained
- Forms Can Reveal Much About an Organization
- Objectives of Forms Management
- Forms Evaluation Starts with Analysis
- Forms Design Follows Analysis
- Printing and Using the Form
- Electronic Forms
- Learning More about Forms Management

CHAPTER 4 45

Writing Format

- Reasons for a Writing Format
- Recommended Writing Format
- Playscript Writing Format for Technical Instructions Only
- Basic Writing Format
- Seven Principal Headings
- Numbering of Headings
- Optional Headings
- Printing (or Copying) Policies and Procedures
- Approval Signatures
- Policy and Procedure Numbers

CHAPTER 5 59

Writing Style

- Effective Writing
- Organization of Thoughts
- Writing Clarity
- Word Meanings
- Jargon

- Spelling, Abbreviations, and Punctuation
- Verb Tenses
- Sentence Structure and Choice of Words
- Gender Words
- Editing

CHAPTER 6 65
Draft Coordination and Approvals
- Rough Draft Phase
- Review Process
- User Review Group
- Management Review Group
- Attorney Review
- Final Approval Authority
- Approval Signatures on Policies and Procedures
- Final Review and Document Sign-off

CHAPTER 7 73
Distribution Methods
- Distribution of Printed and On-line Documents
- Printed Company Manual
- Binder Selection
- Index Tab Dividers
- Sheet Lifters
- Copying the Approved Policy or Procedure
- Distribution Announcement Letter
- Mailing List
- Table of Contents: Numerical, Alphabetical, or Keyword
- Central Repository for Policies and Procedures
- Alternate Methods of Distribution: Company Bulletin, Newsletter, Memorandum, Email, Training

CHAPTER 8 85
Implementation and Training
- Implementation Guidelines
- Control Point
- Benefits of Training
- The Learning Process
- Preparation for Training Classes (15 Points)
- Visual Aids

- Basic Types of Speeches
- Methods of Speaking
- Wording the Speech
- Practicing the Speech
- Delivering the Presentation
- Feedback and Evaluation

CHAPTER 9 103
Revisions
- Revisions to Policies and Procedures
- Research Techniques
- Writing, Coordinating, and Approving the Revised Draft
- Revision History
- Distribution of Revised Policies and Procedures
- Implementation of Revised Policies and Procedures
- Revisions to Revisions

CHAPTER 10 109
On-line Manuals
- On-line Manuals
- Manual Systems Must Precede the On-line System
- Dual Manual System: Printed and On-line
- On-line Documentation: The First Step to Electronic Communication
- The Lure of On-line Documentation
- Benefits of an On-line Manual System
- Designing an On-line Policies and Procedures Manual
- Hypertext
- Clear Writing is Essential
- Converting Printed Manuals

CHAPTER 11 123
Internet and Intranets/Extranets
- Internet
- Intranet
- Extranet
- Linking Policies and Procedures to the Company's Intranet
- Standards of the Intranet
- Converting Printed Manuals for Use on an Intranet

Afterword 134

Bibliography/Recommended Reading 135

Appendices 139
- Core Business Processes
- Sample Content for Policies and Procedures
- Sample Playscript Procedure
- Sample Policy with Indented Numbering
- Sample Policy without Indented Numbering
- Sample Numerical Table of Contents
- Sample Alphabetical Table of Contents
- Sample Policy with Revision History
- Sample On-line Policy Section
- Sample On-line Responsibilities Section
- Sample Intranet Policy/Procedure Template

ABOUT THE AUTHOR

Stephen B. Page is the author of six books, five of which focus on process improvement, business processes, policies, and procedures. Stephen holds a Masters of Business Administration (MBA) in Management from the University of California at Los Angeles (UCLA). He is certified as a project manager (PMP), software engineer (CSQE), records manager (CRM), and forms consultant (CFC).

His employment record contains an impressive list of multinational companies including Nationwide Insurance, Qwest Communications, Boeing Aircraft, Eastman Kodak, and Litton Industries. Stephen has more than 30 years of experience in researching, writing, editing, publishing, communicating, training, measuring, and improving business processes, policies, procedures, and forms. He has written more than 250 company manuals in printed and electronic formats and more than 6000 policies and procedures. He has designed over 4000 forms and has set up manual and electronic form management systems. He has delivered policies and procedures in printed, network, web, and CD-ROM formats. He has had first-hand experience with the application of project management standards, ISO Standards, IEEE Standards, the Capability Maturity Model (CMM), Six Sigma, and the Malcolm Baldrige Award. Stephen has trained thousands of people in the principles of writing effective policies and procedures.

Mr. Page has written many trade journal articles on the subject of process improvement, policies, and procedures, and is a skilled presenter, facilitator, and team leader. He has participated on hundreds of cross-functional team projects. He has lectured at several seminars on the subject of printed and electronic policies and procedures, business processes, process improvement, and forms management.

Mr. Page has worked in various industries including insurance, manufacturing, telecommunications, financial banking, research and development, disaster recovery, software engineering, retail, and general consulting. He has received dozens of awards for his suggestions for various quality programs.

PREFACE

Policies and procedures are like a state road map. The map at a glance shows areas of interest and the general direction in which to travel to reach a desired destination. The roads on the map provide possible paths (choices) to reach a particular destination. If the correct roads are followed, the destination can be reached.

In comparison, a **policy** points out the general direction (objective) to reach a destination (goal) while a **procedure** provides the paths (methods) to accomplish the objectives and goals. The procedure lays out the steps usually followed when performing repeatable types of work.

Challenge to Tradition

Few books have been written that discuss the relationship between business processes, policies, and procedures. The books that attempt to address this subject fall well short of what is most needed by businesses today. This book is unlike any other book available because it contains so much practical information for the procedures analyst. This entire book is devoted to teaching you how to establish a system of policies and procedures based on my successes in several multinational companies.

The heart of this book is the writing format (or outline or structure of writing). It has been successfully used in hundreds of companies and is very easy to understand and apply. After you learn it, it becomes just a matter of filling in the blanks, more or less. It allows you to devote most of your time to establishing a successful system of policies and procedures based on your company's business processes, strategy, and vision.

This book can be used by almost anyone. This is what makes this book so valuable. It is the only book offered on the market today that provides a total solution for establishing a complete policies and procedures system. No other book can make this statement because they do not address such issues as writing format, research, setting up cross-functional teams, working with users and management, converting research to the documentation stage, distribution, implementation, training, or even on-line or Intranet manuals. These are only a few of the practical functions that the procedures analyst should learn.

This book is the first book of a series of policy and procedure book, and serves as the primer as it lays down the foundation needed for the next three books in the series. I wrote this first book in the early 1980's when I had the good fortune to have worked in several large companies where we were given the seemingly impossible task of developing a new system of policies and procedures. I used this as an opportunity to implement the system of policies and procedures that is now the core of this book.

The second book, "7 Steps to Better Written Policies and Procedures" is a "how-to" book that focuses on the use of a structured writing format for policies and procedures. The third book, "Best Practices in Policies and Procedures" focuses on two themes: (1) on the alignment of policies and procedures to the vision, strategic direction, and core processes of policies and procedures; and (2) on developing CONTENT for actual policies and procedures. The fourth book, "Achieving 100% Compliance of Policies and Procedures" focuses on the improvement of business processes and published policies and procedures through improved communications, training, and monitoring programs; auditing and compliance programs; and metrics and measurements for achieving 100% compliance. These four books are best read in the above sequential order.

Overview of the Contents

This book can be used by any size of business in any industry. I try to cover a multitude of subjects necessary to develop printed manuals and electronic manuals for a local area network (LAN) and for an Intranet. The reader is led from researching the company's core business processes to the actual writing, approval, publication, implementation, training, and revision of policies and procedures. A successful writing format is recommended as the basis for writing policies and procedures in the printed, on-line, and Intranet/Extranet formats that will be acceptable to companies worldwide and should meet the necessary requirements for the ISO 9000 Series or the Capability Maturity Model (CMM). As the table of contents is comprehensive, an index has not been included.

INTRODUCTION:
WHO IS THIS BOOK FOR?

The policies and procedures professional, team leader, first-line supervisor, manager, strategic planner, project manager, computer professional, technical writer, trainer, forms professional, or anyone who wants to establish a successful policies and procedures system will find this book very helpful. In fact, this is the only book of its type in which a successful writing format is presented that is easy to learn and apply to new or existing policies and procedures for printed and electronic formatted policies and procedures. My goal is to help you to understand the techniques that you will need to successfully set up and write a successful system of policies and procedures.

I do this by showing you how to develop a successful system of policies and procedures from as early as (1) presenting convincing arguments to your management for establishing a new, or revised, policies and procedures to (2) participating on cross-functional teams to develop the core business processes and policy and procedure topics to (3) writing the content of the actual policy or procedure document to (4) publishing, implementing, training, and revising policies and procedures. I also include chapters on developing on-line manuals and on incorporating printed policies and procedures into an Intranet web site.

Employees of all sizes of companies will find this book worthwhile for many diverse reasons. For example, anyone involved with work flow and efficiency should find this book interesting. While small companies still use printed policies and procedures, larger companies are turning to on-line manuals and the use of the Intranet/Extranet (internal and external websites) for communicating to their employees. Computer professionals will find this book useful when they work with departments to convert printed policies and procedures to network or web manuals.

While the needs of management are different from those that actually write policies and procedures, they are still interested in the detail of the policies and operating procedures. While they may be involved in the writing and afterwords the implementation of the policies and procedures, their primary interest will be in their interpretation.

Terms Used Throughout the Book

1. *He* instead of the awkward *he* or *she*.
2. *CEO/President* instead of distinguishing between the two positions.
3. *Senior management* instead of upper or top-level or any other term that could designate management.
4. *Procedures analyst* instead of policies and procedures analyst or any other term suggested in this book.
5. *Business Process* is a sequence of steps performed for a given purpose, for instance, the software development process. A process is any activity or group of activities that taken an input, adds value to it, and provides an output to an internal or external customer. A process is always behind every policy or procedure. For example, a process could be "write procedures." The policy will give the company's business rules for writing procedures; the procedure will give the details for accomplishing the business rules.
6. *Policy* is a general strategy or purpose. A policy supports a business process.
7. *Procedure* is a plan of action for achieving a policy; it is a method by which a policy can be accomplished and it provides the instructions needed to carry out a policy.

Chapter 1

THE NEED FOR POLICIES AND PROCEDURES

Strategic Role of Policies and Procedures

Policies and procedures play a strategic role in a company environment in which employees make decisions. Policies and procedures become the media by which business processes are documented and published. Through a well-conceived policy and procedure system, the company's vision becomes an integral part of company operations. These operations are the day-to-day planning and decision making which guide the processes of development, manufacturing, distribution, marketing, sales, and servicing of an organization's products or services.

Policies and procedures provide decision-makers with limits, alternatives, and general guidelines. They help to make instructions definite, provide a common understanding of a policy interpretation, and provide quick settlement of misunderstandings. Policies set boundary conditions so that actions and decisions are channeled along a particular path in pursuit of an objective. Policies allow management to operate without constant intervention and, once established, enable others to work within that framework. Policies and procedures need to be in a standard format because they cover recurring situations or processes. They help reduce the range of individual decisions and encourage management by exception. The manager only needs to give special attention to unusual problems not covered by a specific policy or procedure. As more policies and procedures are written to cover recurring situations, managers will begin to make decisions that will be consistent from one functional area to the next. Consistent and objective decisions should be the goals of all companies. They often reflect vision in action and will aid the integration of a company's strategic goals into day-to-day management decisions. Aligning policies and procedures to the vision is straightforward.

It Becomes a Simple Process . . .

A vision is formulated, business processes are analyzed, and the policy and procedure system to support the vision, is born. As policies and procedures are written, approved, published, and implemented, the company's vision is articulated. As the vision is communicated, managers have more control over the future direction of the company and workers have more confidence in job growth and stability. Now as the company grows, so does its vision, and the "writing" process continues.

The fourth book of the series on policies and procedures, "Best Practices in Policies and Procedures" details a method for aligning your policies and procedures to the company's vision, strategic plan, and core processes.

Policy and Procedure Definitions

Understanding the meaning of a *policy* or *procedure* will prove to be a major step in using these terms properly. A POLICY is a "predetermined course of action established as a guide toward accepted business strategies and objectives." A PROCEDURE is a "method by which a policy can be accomplished; it provides the instructions necessary to carry out a policy statement." Policies and procedures do take on other names and these will be addressed in the next section. Each procedure has an action, decision, or repetition step. Additionally, there is always a starting point (initial conditions) and an ending point (goal).

Different Names for Policies and Procedures

I have seen synonyms such as strategies, goals, or objectives for the term *policy*, but I still prefer the traditional word, *policy*. Procedures can take a variety of names depending on the usage, industry, or regulation affected. For example, many departments will use terms like "Standard Operating Procedure" (SOP) "Department Operating Procedure" (DOP) or "Quality Operating Procedure" (QOP). Procedures may be called desk operating procedures or work standards. Whatever the term used, it should be kept in mind that these are general documents written to guide (policies) and to carry out the details of a business process. In some companies, there may be no distinction between a policy and procedure. And in some, there will be a separation of policy and procedure manuals.

It is often the type of industry, the experience of management, or a certification process such as ISO 9000 Quality Standards, Capability Maturity Model (CMM), or Baldrige Award, which establish the type of policies, procedures, and processes defined. While it may seem like any one of these sources has their own unique way of developing a policy and procedure system, the basic terms *policies* and *procedures*, will prevail. This point has been overly emphasized due to the importance of helping you realize that this book gives you the tools necessary to write and develop any kind of policy and procedure system for any company, for any industry, or for any standard imposed on your company.

The business organization should ensure that the content of the policies and procedures does not deliberately violate the various rules, regulations, and laws under which business entities operate. Antitrust laws, banking acts, fair labor standards, tax laws, Medicare, Social Security, transportation laws, and tariff laws are among the various aspects of controls and regulations under which business is conducted.

The procedures analyst should consider the laws and regulations of the country where the policies and procedures are being written. For example, if you write policies and procedures for Saudi Arabia while working for a company in the United States, the laws of Saudi Arabia and not those of the United States need to be considered when writing your policy and procedure documents.

A Delicate Balancing Act

As you can see, the job of writing policies and procedures can be a delicate balancing act. It takes the right personality and experience to write policies and procedures and to be successful at it. This book will teach you the tools necessary to become successful.

3

Internal Control System
Why Policies and Procedures are Needed

One of the most difficult questions to answer is why companies need policies and procedures when they have been operating for years without them. Many companies rely solely upon verbal instructions or a series of company memoranda. An irrefutable answer to this question will be explained in the next few pages. This answer is meant to be used as ammunition for those who struggle with obtaining management approval and support for creating a policy and procedure system.

The Answer - Technical Explanation

The answer to the aforementioned question is based on the relationship between a company's internal control system and its organizational structure. The successful operation of an organization is dependent on an effective system of internal controls. A valid control system can assure that commands are being carried out as required and warn the central decision-making function of changes in circumstances that require new sets of commands.

In a corporate organization, management installs whatever internal controls it considers vital and necessary to the continued well-being of the company; the controls exist for and because of management. The internal control system is concerned with all aspects that contribute to the existence and well-being of an organization, in which case, management assures itself that actions taken by its employees conform to its policies and procedures.

Three Internal Controls

There are three internal controls that are essentially the same in all business organizations. Sample core business processes and policies and procedures that could satisfy an internal control system are referenced in Appendices A and B. These controls are described below:

1. *Administrative Controls* are non-financial and encompass all business activities. They are concerned with operational efficiency and with the

adherence to managerial policies. These controls are involved with the decision-making processes that precede management's authorization of transactions.

2. *Accounting Controls* are financial and provide the checks and balances in the accounting system to:

   a. Prevent errors before transactions (sales, purchases, cash receipts, cash disbursements, or payroll) are recorded;

   b. Detect and correct errors in the accounting records; and

   c. Safeguard the company's assets.

3. *Data Processing Controls* may overlap both administrative and accounting controls or they involve the input, processing, and output of computerized transactions.

Organizational Structure for Policies and Procedures

The organization should provide for the coordination of all personnel so that the company's goals and objectives will be met. Management uses the knowledge, talents, and wisdom of its personnel to accomplish these objectives. It is through this team effort that internal control is achieved. An organizational structure provides the framework within which decisions are made. The work of an organization is divided so that each officer, traditionally, a manager reporting directly to the chief executive officer, has the authority to act in a given area of activity. These activities may include sales, marketing, finance, customer service, accounting, engineering, personnel relations, production, and quality control.

Responsibilities for specific tasks are assigned to functional areas and limits of authority are established for competent and trustworthy employees. The effectiveness of a business organization depends on having an adequate number of competent and honest employees to do work at each level. Qualified and reliable employees help to create an appropriate internal control environment.

Responsibility refers to an individual who is entitled to act on his own accord. It is the commitment of subordinates to their superiors in performing the duties of their jobs. It is the obligation of a subordinate to achieve the desired conditions for which he is accountable to his superiors. *Authority* refers to an individual who has the right to take action and make decisions. Authority in management constitutes a form of influence and a right to take action, to direct and coordinate the actions of others, and to use discretion in the position he occupies. The delegation of authority allows decisions to be made more rapidly by those who are in more direct contact with the problem.

The segregation of duties and the establishment of clearly defined authorizations are necessary to ensure a checks and balances system, thus ensuring that no one person handles all phases of a transaction from beginning to end. Ideally, the flow of activities should be designed so that the work of one employee either is independent of or serves as a check on the work of another. It is necessary for management to define who should do what so the work to be done is carried out. It is not cost effective to have duplicate responsibilities, or gaps in responsibility, since both could lead to conflict or tasks not being done at all.

The management of an organization is responsible for making employees aware that policies and procedures will be monitored and that failure to follow the established guidelines will be detected. To assure the cooperation of subordinates, it is important that authorization levels are realistic and consistent with the importance of the matter, as well as with the responsibilities of the people concerned.

Policies and Procedures Define Employee Roles

Policies create expectations and guides for action. Procedures provide the means by which the actions can be carried out by management and by employees. The segregation of duties established within the organizational structure can be used as a guide when writing policies and procedures for assigning specific responsibilities and tasks to employees and functional areas. Once responsibilities have been assigned, policies and procedures take on meaning as responsible individuals are assigned important tasks within the workflow. These are the people who can make the policies and procedures work.

Policies and Procedures are Considered
Internal Controls

Well-conceived guidelines that satisfy internal controls will ensure a continual coordination of group efforts within the organization toward the achievement of company goals and objectives. Company goals and objectives cannot be achieved when consistency and continuity are lacking in management decisions. Without policies and procedures, this group effort may not materialize because management and employees would have to regularly reinterpret routine and recurring situations.

Policies and procedures are considered internal controls because they play a decisive role in reducing intentional or unintentional exposure to errors in those accounting records and reports used for the management of funds, determining the accountability of assets, and the making of decisions that affect both the internal environment of the organization and the external world.

Eight Reasons for Documenting Policies and Procedures

Besides the technical reasons previously explained, there are many other reasons for documenting policies and procedures. These include, but are not limited to:

1. Every job has constraints surrounding it. Without written policies and procedures, employees would be on their own to discover these constraints by trial and error. The organization would become disorganized and its managers would not have the means to direct and harmonize their staff's activities.
2. Policies and procedures enable managers and their subordinates to clearly understand the individual and group responsibilities including the boundaries within which they have to work and the demands upon them.
3. Policies and procedures set clear boundaries for jobs so that each employee knows in advance what response he will get from others when making decisions.
4. Policies and procedures create a baseline to which subsequent change can be referred and through which the way things are done is enabled.

5. Policies and procedures enable managers to decide whether a subordinate's improper action or decision was due simply to poor judgment or to an infringement of the rules. If no rules exist, the subordinate cannot be criticized for using his judgment, however poorly he may use it. If a rule exists, management has to establish whether it was accidentally or deliberately broken, for the latter is a disciplinary offense. Without written policies and procedures, employees would not know where they stand and any decision may create an unwanted precedent.

6. Policies and procedures provide individuals the freedom to make decisions in the execution of their duties within defined boundaries and to help avoid over-control by managers. If people are uncertain about the limits of their job, they cannot feel free to act.

7. Policies and procedures enable management to exercise control by exception rather than by every action and decision of their subordinates.

8. Policies and procedures enable managers to control events in advance. Before the action begins, employees know the rules and are more likely to produce the right result the first time. Without policies and procedures, management is forced to control events after they happen and the results may cause dissatisfaction. Alternatively, a manager must be on the scene of the event to respond when the situation approaches its limits. This is a costly use of a manager's time.

Managing the Policies and Procedures Function

Once it has been decided that a policy and procedure system is required, it should be determined who should manage and coordinate this function. Typically, the CEO/President of the business organization will appoint a single department to manage this important responsibility. This department would be empowered to recommend policies and procedures that express the thinking of senior management. As we will see, in reality, the policies and procedures that are often recommended to senior management for approval, are the result of the efforts of teams working with users and management to find mutually-acceptable solutions that result in written documentation.

8

While it may not seem important where the department reports to, it may make a huge difference in terms of company recognition and how quickly a new process is approved and accepted by those who use it or are affected by it. It is highly preferable for the policies and procedures department to report to the person with final approval authority. *Final approval authority* refers to the last signature required for a policy or procedure. Ideally, this is the CEO/President of a company. While titles and organizational structures may be different, this is one of the best reporting structures for the policies and procedures department in terms of authority and recognition purposes.

If the procedures analyst reports to a lower-level manager who, in turn, reports directly to the person with final approval authority, there could be a problem of mixed loyalties and miscommunication about final content. The advice of a lower-level manager may be different from the advice of the person who makes the final approvals. If the procedures analyst is to maintain objectivity, he needs to report directly to the final signature authority, or at least, have access to this person.

The person with the final approval authority is also the one who can provide the procedures department with guidance in developing policies and procedures and/or in resolving departmental conflicts over ideas, suggestions, or rough drafts. It seems appropriate, therefore, that the procedures department report directly to the final approval authority for all policies and procedures.

If this kind of reporting structure cannot be achieved, or is not possible, then the following guidelines should be considered:

1. The CEO/President should authorize the establishment, and ongoing maintenance, of a policies and procedures system.
2. The CEO/President should issue a letter designating both the departments responsible for the policies and procedures function and an individual responsible for final approval authority. This person could be a senior person in Finance or Human Resources.
3. It should become a general practice that proposed policies and procedures be reviewed by both senior management and the CEO/President before being distributed and implemented.

Six Decisions for the
Policies and Procedures Department

If the policies and procedures system is just being initiated, or if major changes are needed in an existing system, there are at least six important decisions that need to be addressed.

1. What will be the number of distinctly named manuals (policy, procedure, or departmental) allowed in this policy or procedure system?
2. What are the vision, mission, and strategic objectives for the company, and more specifically, for the policies and procedures department?
3. What is the format that will be used for writing and collecting information for the manuals?
4. What will be the role of forms management?
5. What types of persons will be hired as procedures analysts?
6. What is the content for these manuals?

Company Manuals
FIRST Decision

The type of manual is the first decision. The answer to this decision is dependent on the size of the company, the budget committed to this project, and any particular industry or governmental regulations that might have influence over some of the guidelines expressed in policies and procedures. There could be policies and procedures for each department or one policy manual for the corporation and many procedure manuals for each department, or even a combination of manuals.

One or two volumes of a manual covering all general policies and procedures for the company is preferable. This manual would have sections for each department and would have both policy and procedure documents in one manual. The policies would be printed on blue paper and the procedures on white paper. This is basically the system discussed throughout this book. Each department would also be permitted to have their own procedure manual as long as their estimate of policies and procedures for their area exceeds five documents.

As a company grows in both revenues and employees, the number of policies and procedures should grow to meet this demand. A small company with 100 people may have one manual covering all functions within a company. Whereas a larger company of 500 people could have an overall administrative manual with several departmental manuals. This selection of the type and number of manuals is a key question and should be carefully reviewed by both the policies and procedures department and by the senior management of the company. The number of manuals may also be dependent on the company's philosophy toward being certified as ISO 9000 compliant, being accessed at one of the five maturity levels of the Capability Maturity Model (CMM), or meeting the criteria of the Baldrige Award.

Goals and Objectives
SECOND Decision

The sooner the Policies and Procedures Department can achieve a reputation for success, the easier it will be to implement new guidelines. Besides being successful in developing policies and procedures, reputation can be enhanced if the Policies and Procedures Department displays its vision, mission, and objectives. These should be written according to the company's vision and mission statement. The Policies and Procedures Department should be proud to display its vision and mission. As this is a subject for an entire series of books, obtaining books on writing vision and mission statements from the library or local bookstore is suggested.

Role of Forms Management
THIRD Decision

A third decision concerns the question of whether the management of forms should be an integral part of the policies and procedures function. Although this matter is often overlooked, forms management plays an important role in a company's operations. Forms are tools that are used to communicate, request something, answer a question, etc.

> A form is a business process in work.

Forms provide an efficient and economical way to write instructions and control actions in business.

The forms analyst and the procedures analyst should work very closely in coordinating procedures with forms. There is a tremendous need to simplify forms and thereby simplify the activities of employees. Through forms, employees' jobs can be made easier and faster. A forms analyst is interested in how a system functions as it relates to forms and supporting forms. The activities of the forms analyst are similar to those of the procedures analyst. Both individuals analyze and design working systems. In fact, typically, both persons could be concerned with the same system at the same time.

If the control for both forms and procedures is in one department, it is far easier to coordinate the distribution of a newly approved policy or procedure with the distribution of a newly manufactured form. The functions of these two analysts are so similar that they often work closely together; this similarity of responsibility and research topics functions well when they work alongside each other in the same department.

Often, in small companies, the procedures and forms analyst are one in the same. In larger companies, the forms analyst may report to the procedures function. In very large companies, the forms analyst may work in a Forms Management Department and that department could report to the Procedures Department. It is possible for these two functions to be separate within the company but it has been proven by experience, that the best working relationship is when the forms manager is also the procedures manager or when the forms analyst works for, or closely, with the procedures analyst.

Types of Persons Hired
FOURTH Decision

The fourth decision concerns the selection of persons to work within the policies and procedures department. At a minimum, there should be a manager. If the budget is small, the manager will probably become the procedures analyst. As the function grows, procedures analysts should be added to this department. These individuals would perform the following kinds of activities:

1. Managing the policy and procedure system for the company or a particular department; becoming the champion for new or revised policies and procedures; participating (or leading) teams or meetings to discuss new, or revised, policies and procedures;
2. Coordinating forms issues with current, past, or planned policies and procedures;
3. Documenting the writing format;
4. Obtaining proper approvals for drafts of policies and procedures and resolving conflicts, when possible;
5. Helping with communication of policies and procedures through training classes and other means of communication; and
6. Coordinating issues and questions about business processes, policies, procedures, and the interpretation of approved policies and procedures, with all levels of the company.

Popular titles for individuals working within the Policies and Procedures Department include:

1. Policy Development Manager
2. Policies and Procedures Analyst or Writer
3. Procedures Analyst or Writer
4. Strategic Planning Officer
5. Business Process Compliance Officer
6. Process Designer or Process Design Consultant

The selection process for finding persons suited for this kind of work may be somewhat simplified by analyzing the type of person most suited for this role. A major decision is whether to hire from within the company or from outside the company.

Hiring from Within the Company

If the procedures analyst is hired from within the company, the fact that this person may have some loyalties to the department from which he came could present a potential problem. There have been situations where someone loyal to a department tries to make things go easier for his fellow employees. In this case, it leads to poorly analyzed and implemented policies and procedures. One advantage of hiring from within the company, on the other hand, is that the current employee normally possesses a large knowledge base about a company's operations.

Hiring from Outside the Company

In every case where I have been involved in the hiring of procedures analysts, it has proven to be a better decision to hire someone from outside the company. It is preferable that this person has worked in a similar industry or has some knowledge of the products or services produced. While this is preferred, it should not be a firm requirement.

One major advantage for hiring from outside the company is that the potential employee hired will have a *fresh* look on your system. This is very important to your policies and procedures system regardless of whether it is an established system or is just being established. A fresh look; someone with new ideas and different methods of operating, will be an asset to your company. An experienced policies and procedures person knows how to identify and analyze business processes and convert this information to actual policies and procedures. Another advantage is the fact that this person is not known by anyone in the company. It is amazing how much progress a new person can make. The new person has not had time to learn bad mistakes or to alienate anyone.

Job Specifications for a New Hire

The job specifications for a Procedures Analyst include, but are not limited to:

1. A well-rounded education and a business process background;
2. Team facilitation and meeting skills;
3. Analytical, organized, and efficient;
4. Able to communicate with all levels of the company;
5. Even disposition and able to withstand pressure;
6. Supervisory skills;
7. Writing ability and familiarity with forms;
8. Strong drive to succeed; and
9. Work experience of at least five years.

14

Content Determination
FIFTH Decision

The suggested topics for policies and procedures of a new system need to be determined before any work can begin. For existing systems, the content of revisions and/or new policies and procedures needs to be decided before much activity can take place. Included is an extensive discussion of content determination in Chapter 2 as well as sample core business processes and policies and procedures topics in the appendices. The subject of finding content for a policy or procedure is the subject of another book in the series on policies and procedures called, "Best Practices in Policies and Procedures."

Writing Format
SIXTH Decision

The writing format recommended in this book is the subject of Chapter 4. Only one writing format is recommended because it has proven to be very successful in many companies including several multinational companies. This writing format will become the format of all your future policies and procedures. I have also suggested that you consider using the Playscript writing format for technical manuals. This writing format is the subject of another book in the series on policies and procedures called, "7 Steps to Better Written Policies and Procedures."

Summary

Policies and procedures play a strategic role in a company environment in which employees make decisions. Uniformity, consistency, and conformity can be assured because company personnel are expected to become familiar with and follow written policies and procedures. When policies and procedures are finally communicated to all those affected, the process can begin for assuring that employees comply with applicable responsibilities and authorizations.

In this chapter, we have established an irrefutable argument for a system of policies and procedures. Guidelines for establishing a policies and procedures department have been set forth and a plan for hiring procedures professionals has been defined. References have been provided for locating additional information about the subjects contained in this chapter.

Chapter 2

RESEARCH METHODS

Importance of Research to a
Policies and Procedures System

Research is a critical activity in establishing a successful policies and procedures system. It is a function that is required every time a policy, procedure, or process is begun or revisited. Whether you call it research, investigation, or the gathering of information, the main goal is to discover and interpret the facts and to find acceptable alternatives to a current problem, process, or document. A secondary goal is to gather information that will be used to create your policy or procedure. The heart of this book, Chapter 4, will explain how to use the information gathered within the recommended writing format.

Target of Research

The source for research will ultimately be the list of new policies and procedures that you derive from an analysis of the core business processes. There are a variety of successful ways to collect the data that will be used in your research efforts. Paramount to further research is the determination of content of in the current or planned policies and procedures manuals. With a list of topics or a list of existing policies and procedures, you are ready to start the research that will help you write your new, or revised, policies and procedures. I will present methods for understanding the current process and for deciding your own list of policies and procedures. With this list you will be able to approach your own management, or the subordinates who report to this management, and discuss the ways to define the detail of these policies and procedures. Thus, your content will take on meaning. Initially, this content will just be a list of possible new, or revised topics.

Determining Content for Manuals

Determining content can be done in several different ways. In this section, I have tried to include a variety of tried-and-proven methods that have been successful for me. These include business process reengineering, benchmarking, networking, and using ideas outlined in the ISO 9000 Quality Standards. I have addressed how to find new, or revised, content for existing policies and procedures and how to find content for a new policies and procedures system. The book, "Best Practices in Policies and Procedures" contains a process for determining content that starts with the vision of the company and continues with the strategic plan, core processes, policy and procedure topics, and concludes with the content of the specific policy or procedure.

EXISTING POLICIES AND PROCEDURES

In the situation where an organization has an existing set of policies and procedures, there will be many cases where new policies and procedures will be required and/or where revisions will need to be made. In both cases, research is an important element because the original business process should be revisited and solutions identified before the change can be properly documented. New, or revised content for existing procedures will follow the same guidelines as determining content for a new policies and procedures system.

Revisions to Policies or Procedures

Often the need for a revision to an existing policy or procedure arises when a process breaks down, or a problem is identified, or when a law or regulation is changed. In these cases, the driving business process will be reviewed first, followed by a study of the specific process that is causing the problem. It might even require a major rewrite of the policy or procedure and perhaps even the entire process could be viewed as a new policy or procedure. The methods for analysis change depending on the action that needs to be taken. For example, in the case of a revision where a new law needs to be incorporated, the change is clear and little additional research is required. However, one consideration that cannot be overlooked is how this new regulation might affect other policies and procedures.

For example, if a new computer system has been set up, it could have major effects on data processing policies and procedures. It becomes the task of the procedures analyst to seek out which existing policies and procedures are affected and what new processes require new policies and procedures to be researched and written.

Business Process Reengineering

Business process reengineering is a method that can be used for revisiting a process. But it is more than that. It does not mean to revise or modify. It means to scrap the old and start over with a blank sheet of paper. While an existing process is needed for measurement purposes, that is the extent of it. Business process reengineering means abandoning long-established procedures and looking afresh at the work required to create a company's product or service and deliver value to the customer. It involves going back to the beginning and inventing a better way of doing work.

One goal of business process reengineering is to get people involved and proud to work with a new process rather than resenting it.

> The result of reengineering a business process is better policies and procedures to carry out the new process.

Often, a result of reengineering is total employee involvement. It becomes a much easier process to carry out new policies and procedures when there is employee support. Business process reengineering is an excellent business tool for researching policies and procedures. It is recommended that you visit a library, a local bookstore, or the Internet to find useful books and other information on this subject. You will find books dedicated to the subject of business process reengineering. During your search process, you should consider looking at topics like business process improvement, total quality management, continuous improvement, or process management.

Creating content is not as difficult as it seems. There are several methods for identifying possible topics for manuals including business process reviews, benchmarking, networking, forms management, or soliciting ideas from management. I will provide sample policies and procedures topics for six areas in Appendix B. Creating content is nothing more than outlining the process involved and determining what should be done, step-by-step. From this exercise, you should arrive at the topics needed for your manuals. Once you review the sample core processes presented in Appendix A and compare them to the sample policies and procedures topics in Appendix B, you should have a better understanding about this collection method.

Additionally, the existence of industry regulations will provide a source of content for your manuals. They could also pose certain restrictions on the actual wording of the policy or procedure. Furthermore, it could be a part of the company's vision to become certified by such standards as the ISO 9000 Quality Series or the Capability Maturity Model (CMM). Each of these standards provides an excellent source for lists of possible procedure topics. For example, the "ISO 9000 Quality System Handbook" referenced in the bibliography contains a section of more than 120 procedural topics that would provide an enormous amount of material for your content list. In this case, it is suggested that this list of topics would more than suffice in meeting ISO 9000 Quality System certification requirements.

Reviewing Core Business Processes

For a new system, a major step would be to identify the core business processes, or those processes that represent the company's major operations. Within each process, there will be many policies and procedures to write. These policies and procedures become the content for the manuals.

Identification of the core business processes is a function for the management of your company. These business processes could be based on the mission and vision statements and will represent the key activities essential to a given organization. Once these core business processes are identified and approved, your task of determining which policies and procedures supports these processes can begin. Examples of business processes for three companies are located in Appendix A. These examples are the actual core business processes of three multinational companies. They will provide a starting point for you. My latest book, "Best Practices in Policies and Procedures" addresses the issue of finding content in more detail. A URL is provided that gives you links to actual policies and procedures used in various companies and organizations.

METHODS TO DETERMINE CONTENT
FOR NEW MANUALS

Once the core business processes are confirmed, approved, and published by your management, there are several good methods for determining a list of policies and procedures to include in your manual. With this list of possible policies and procedures, you will be able to continue to the next step of establishing cross-functional teams to work out the details of, or populate, the policies and procedures. I will teach you methods to extract this information from your current processes and provide you methods for soliciting this information from sources outside your organization.

Benchmarking

Benchmarking is used to establish a baseline for your business processes. It is a method for seeking out the *best practice* and *innovation* in an industry. It is defined as a "continuous, systematic process for evaluating the products, services, and work processes of an organization that has been recognized as representing *best practices* and *innovation* for organizational improvement." It is the process of studying the best practices of well-run, world-class companies to establish operating targets for your company. With benchmarking, you can accelerate the rate of improvement in your organization and provide the rationale for both continuous improvement and strategic quality planning.

Benchmarking is not limited to external organizations. It can be used within a company as well. For example, there may be one department in your company that has been exemplary in all aspects. This department could be used as a model for other departments. Many organizations recognize immediate gains by identifying their best internal processes and transferring that information to other parts of their organization.

Benchmarking is an excellent thinking and investigative tool. It becomes a powerful tool for procedures analysts because it helps them communicate more with other areas of the company and with other companies. You can use benchmarking for new or existing policies and procedures.

If you decide that benchmarking is a tool that will be used by your company, it is recommended that you thoroughly understand your own processes before venturing out to other departments or other companies. It will not only give you an excellent perspective to work from, but it will also help with your credibility. When using any new tool, it is good to make sure that you understand the tool and not be embarrassed by it.

Networking

Networking, or interacting with others with similar interests, is an excellent method for soliciting ideas about policies and procedures ideas from different companies. Networking contacts come from a variety of sources including training classes, symposiums, and business meetings. Even a casual discussion in a restaurant can prove fruitful. A little camaraderie can go a long way when you need someone to talk with; and that business card can become a new source of information. In this case, you would be seeking any kind of help or reference material that the other company would be willing to share with you. Sometimes you may get a copy of a complete manual. Other times, the contact can probably steer you in the right direction and possibly provide names and contacts within their own organization and in local associations.

It is also useful to join and participate in local associations involved with office administration, records, and forms. Often these organizations encompass many administrative-type individuals who can serve as an excellent source of information. Both the records and forms associations encompass all areas of business and thus many of those attending these association meetings and seminars will be interested in the same kinds of issues as your company. Two popular associations are the Business Forms Management Association (BFMA) located at http://www.bfma.org/ and the Administration of Records Managers Association (ARMA) located at http://www.arma.org/. Membership in almost any association can prove fruitful as contacts can become a good source of information. If the association has a newsletter, journal, or magazine, often you can find archived articles that can meet your needs.

Coordinating Ideas with Forms Management

As forms and procedures go hand in hand, seeking information from the company's forms management personnel will prove to be very helpful. A form is "a procedure, or process in action," and forms management may already have analyzed some of the processes in which you are interested. If forms have been created for a particular process, then forms management should have done some analysis to design these forms. If forms does not exist for particular processes, then the procedures analyst can use this opportunity to work closely with forms management to understand this process. As we will see in Chapter 3, forms management plays a very important role in the execution of most functions in an organization.

Obtaining Ideas from Management

Questioning management on policies and procedures topics can prove to be very valuable. The management of a specific department or a manager with many years of experience at your company, could be an excellent source of information. I have seen many cases where a manager in an unrelated department has acquired useful experience, though not used in his present capacity, which can be beneficial to providing valuable insights into the development of a system of policies and procedures.

This investigative process can be done with a letter, email, or in person. Each way has its advantages and disadvantages. I would recommend a combination of techniques including writing a letter, an email with questions, and setting up one-on-one meetings. You need to establish solid rapport that is long-lasting. This personal meeting can give you an excellent chance to make an impression and get on a manager's good side. You will need his support later.

It can also be effective to set up brainstorming sessions with the management of various departments. The result of these sessions will be a list of new, or revised policies and procedures, and maybe some that could be considered obsolete. This is an excellent technique for soliciting unbiased ideas from many company personnel. Brainstorming will be discussed further in this chapter when I address cross-functional teams.

External Sources that Influence Content: ISO 9000 Series and Capability Maturity Model

There can be several regulations, standards, or certifications that will provide solid leads to policies and procedures topics. In banking and insurance industries, there are regulations that can give you an idea of the content that is required for your manuals. For software companies, there is an important standard called Capability Maturity Model (CMM) that can give you clues to content. The ISO 9000 Quality Series is another worldwide standard that can be applied to any industry. Another major influence could be your company's participation in the Malcolm Baldrige National Quality Award. A well-established system of policies and procedures could be a deciding factor in qualifying for this award. Whole books have been written on this subject, so I suggest that you do your own research as well as refer to my bibliography.

There are other external sources that may affect the way you develop and write your policies and procedures. If your company has an attorney, or if your company retains one, it could prove very helpful to consult him regarding your plans for establishing a system of policies and procedures. It can also prove beneficial to discuss your ideas with the senior Financial Officers. If you can gain the support of these people, you will find many doors opened to you as you move forward in your efforts to establish a policies and procedures system.

The ISO 9000 Series of Standards

The ISO 9000 SERIES is a set of documents dealing with quality systems in all industries. They specify requirements and recommendations for the design and assessment of a management system with the purpose of ensuring that suppliers provide products and services that satisfy specified requirements. These quality standards clarify the distinctions and interrelationships of quality ideas and provide guidelines for the selection or use of a set of 20 international standards on quality systems. These standards encompass all processes within a company. Each requires that policies and procedures be documented, understood, carried out, and maintained. They also require that responsibilities and authorities for all personnel specifying and monitoring quality be defined, and that in-house verification of resources be defined, trained, and funded. While these standards provide a direction to follow, they do not provide the actual wording or format of the suggested policies, procedures, or work instructions. One of the greatest values of this book is that it includes a successful writing standard that is acceptable to these external standards, certifications, and regulations.

Typically, the ISO 9000 Series requires three types of manuals for its documentation: (1) policies; (2) procedures; and (3) work instructions and/or form instructions. Depending on the size of the company, there is generally one companywide manual for policies, one procedure manual for each department, and one or more manuals for working instructions as required to support the procedure manuals. Registrars, or those companies that certify qualified companies as ISO 9000 compliant, are generally flexible in what they approve. They should be consulted early in your plan to become compliant. If you follow the general guidelines set forth in this book, coupled with the registrar's recommendations, your company should have no problem becoming certified.

ISO 9000 Standards provide a great start for policies and procedures systems because they are one of the few documented sources that I am aware of providing a listing of possible procedure topics that will produce an effective policies and procedures system. ISO 9000 Quality Standards are only a beginning. They provide a mechanism to cause systematic improvement. Additional information can be obtained from your local library or bookstore.

The CMM Process

The CAPABILITY MATURITY MODEL (CMM) process was developed by the Scientific Engineering Institute (SEI) and is a framework that describes the key elements of an effective software process. The CMM for software is one of the best-known products of this institute. The CMM is powerful because it provides the detail necessary to understand the requirements of each maturity level, and as such permits you to examine your practices and see how they compare with one another. You can then identify any gaps and establish improvement priorities to address your particular needs. CMM guides software organizations in selecting process improvement strategies by deciding their current process maturity and identifying the few issues most critical to improving their software process. CMM is a description of the five maturity levels through which software organizations evolve as they define, implement, measure, control, and improve their software processes. At each level, there are many policies and procedures that are required before advancing to the next level. For further information about CMM contact:

Software Engineering Institute
Carnegie Mellon University
Pittsburgh, PA 15213-3890
(412) 268-5800

http://www.sei.cmu.edu/sei-home.html

Both the CMM and the ISO 9000 Series are important industry standards that represent the most sought after quality standards for companies. They are not only important to companies in terms of improving their processes but they also represent an excellent source for policies and procedures content. It should be mentioned that even if your company is not pursuing these disciplines, it could prove most useful to purchase several books (see bibliography) on the subject as an aid to determine topics for possible policies and procedures topics.

Determining the Details behind Policies and Procedures

With a list of policies and procedures topics in hand, the first step in developing policies and procedures has been accomplished. The next step is to determine the detail behind each topic. Total cooperation among departments is necessary to minimize inconsistencies from the standpoint of overall company policy. The procedures analyst can bring together individuals with various responsibilities and expertise for interviews and to form teams. The more involved the participants are in the visits, interviews, or meetings, the easier it will be to implement the policy or procedure.

Cross-Functional Teams

As the procedures analyst moves forward in the development of the policies and procedures system, he will discover that the use of teams whose membership crosses departmental lines will be most beneficial in expediting the completion, implementation, and participation in policies and procedures. These special teams are called *cross-functional teams* and are composed of those individuals from departments within the organization whose competencies are essential to each area. The variety of experiences, backgrounds, and skill sets will increase the probability of creativity within the group. These teams will reduce the time it takes to get things accomplished and they will help to improve the organization's ability to solve complex issues through the use of the essential core competencies of its diverse group of employees. The development of this team should not be haphazard, but rather carefully planned. My book, "Best Practices in Policies and Procedures" provides extensive details into the operation of cross-functional teams.

Team Purpose

The purpose of cross-functional team meetings will be to exchange, brainstorm ideas, and diagram the proposed new, or revised, process, policy, or procedure. The primary objectives are to: (1) define a particular subject to the satisfaction of the users; (2) examine all reasonable alternate courses of actions; and (3) unanimously select one alternative that will be used as the basis for the proposed policy or procedure.

Team Leadership

While most teams with which you are familiar have a team leader that is either assigned by management or elected by the team members, the policies and procedures cross-functional team is different. In this case, the goals and objectives are clear and it is often the policies and procedures department that requests certain policies and procedures be evaluated and published. With the right background and skills, the procedures analyst often makes an excellent leader especially because he is completely focused on ensuring total implementation and compliance of business processes, policies, and procedures.

With a strong business process and workflow background, the procedures analyst can bring the team together because he:

1. Asks questions that bring out ideas and stimulate discussion;
2. Uses paraphrasing and other listening skills;
3. Manages the group discussion;
4. Establishes an informal, relaxed atmosphere;
5. Uses consensus method to reach decisions on key team issues;
6. Involves members in setting the goals and objectives of the team;
7. Implements good team meeting guidelines including an agenda, use of a facilitator, note taker, and time keeper;
8. Insists that team members respect each other and that each person's contributions are valued; and
9. Celebrates the achievement of team milestones.

Once the system of policies and procedures is established, departments will start seeking ways to make improvements. In this case, they should invite the procedures analyst to become a member of their team.

Selecting Team Players

When selecting teams, the procedures analyst should discuss the team membership with senior management to affirm their endorsement of both the team and the members being selected. Perhaps the most important criteria for a cross-functional team is to select at least one person from each area affected by the proposed policy or procedure. Ideal team players will have the following qualifications:

1. Responsible and motivated for finding solutions to problems;
2. Relevant expertise;
3. Know how to find and obtain data or technical advice;
4. Can be trusted to be liberal-minded;
5. View themselves as playing a major role and as someone who cares;

6. Willing to participate and be open-minded during a team setting; and
7. Willing to cooperate during a team meeting.

Teams should be relatively small. You might want to start with a core of 4-8 individuals. As the subject discussions continue, you may consider subteams that report to the main team. The leader of these subteams does not have to be the procedures analyst but it is a preferred practice.

If the procedures analyst is not the leader, he should be one of the members of the team. It is his job to ensure that a reasonable solution is reached and that the policy or procedure is documented. The procedures analyst should make it a point to attend all of the policy and procedure meetings including the subteam meetings, where possible.

Conducting Meetings and Selecting Meeting Topics

The procedures analyst will ensure that team meetings are scheduled at least once a week until the policy or procedure has been documented. The procedures analyst will set up the time, place, and day. He will send out a meeting notice to all members of the team. He will attach an agenda for review before the meeting and ask for additional topics to be addressed.

It is important to ask members of the team to come prepared to the meeting. If the subject of the meeting is known far enough in advance, the participants will have time enough to prepare. If possible, it can be most helpful if the input can be collected and distributed before the meeting. This activity will reduce meeting time.

The first meeting of any policy and procedure team should address the meeting rules for the team activities. These include:

1. Identifying purpose and a method to measure progress;
2. Defining a charter and ground rules;
3. Assigning a minutes taker, time keeper, and possibly a facilitator;
4. Setting up an issues bin;
5. Agreeing to do periodic feedback sessions;
6. Agreeing on milestones and meeting closure dates;
7. Determining if any of the team members need additional training to be effective participants; and
8. Defining what will make the team successful.

Subsequent meetings can be devoted to accomplishing goals including:

1. Describing the current process flow, both visually and textually;
2. Measuring the process in terms of new process objectives;
3. Assessing the process in terms of new process attributes;
4. Identifying problems with, or shortcomings of, the process;
5. Identifying short-term improvements to the process;
6. Assessing current information technology and organization;
7. Concentrating on streamlining the process to:
   a. Eliminate bureaucracy and red tape;
   b. Eliminate duplication of effort and unnecessary forms;
   c. Eliminate process bottlenecks;
   d. Simplify the job and the skill-level requirements;
   e. Give employees end-to-end responsibility for a job assignment;
   f. Use automation.

Selection of Alternate Solutions

The selection of alternate solutions is an important part of the team meeting experience. The group needs to mutually agree on one alternative. The team can use brainstorming, company employee "experts," internal or external benchmarking, or business process reengineering techniques. The use of automation can be explored. Vendors can be contacted for assistance if specific products are being discussed. There are many ways to explore and develop solutions to alternatives. This exploration effort could take weeks, months, or even years. Once a choice is made, the team can concentrate on defining the process and work toward a rough draft of the policy or the procedure. The cross-functional team will continue to assist the procedures analyst until the policy or procedure is distributed and implemented.

Developing the Selected Alternate Solution

Brainstorming Ideas

The team should consider using brainstorming as a primary means of soliciting ideas from one another. *Brainstorming* refers to any group facilitation technique or practice that encourages participation from all group members, whatever their roles and relationships within the organization. Emphasis during brainstorming sessions should be on creativity and idea generation. A nonjudgmental atmosphere is essential. Any idea should be fair game. The goals should be to (1) brainstorm design alternatives; (2) assess feasibility, risk, and the benefit of design alternatives (3) select the preferred process design and develop a migration strategy; and (4) set up new organizational structures and designs. Brainstorming sessions usually produce many design alternatives. This is an excellent team exercise that will result in many process ideas for policies and procedures.

Research Outside the Team Meeting

During team meetings, there will be cause to invite employees with knowledge of specific subjects to participate in a meeting. Sometimes this practice will not prove timely and it will be necessary to meet with various employees off-line. In these cases, both the procedures analyst and the team members may have to conduct one-on-one meetings, telephone calls, and questionnaires to obtain the information for a particular process. Interviewing skills might include, but are not limited, to:

1. Gathering necessary facts;
2. Making interviewees feel they make a difference;
3. Interviewing in the work setting, if possible;
4. Asking for full descriptions to your answers;
5. Asking for any pertinent procedures, process descriptions that add to what you already have;
6. Immediately after the interview, writing up what you were told so you remember details; and
7. Developing a network of resource people.

Telephone Interviews

Telephone interviews are sometimes used for informal meetings, especially when the information should be collected quickly and inexpensively, and the amount of information required is limited. The telephone interview has advantages besides speed and economy. It is frequently easier to get the cooperation of people over the telephone than in a meeting. People tend to talk very freely and candidly on the telephone. This can be an especially good way to talk with people who get nervous in front of crowds. The main disadvantage is the limited amount of information that can be obtained. Also, it is not always clear if the person on the other end of the telephone is really paying attention. It is not always easy to determine body language on a telephone.

Questionnaires

If all the users do not work in one location or even within one city or within one state, a written questionnaire could be prepared to solicit information. A questionnaire is actually an interview on paper. These questionnaires could be mailed out to the users. Care needs to be taken to ensure that the questionnaire contains questions that are easy to understand and hard to misinterpret. Mail questionnaires provide great versatility at relatively low cost. Some serious drawbacks to mail questionnaires are the problems of nonresponse and the inability of the procedures analyst to ensure that questions are fully understood and properly sequenced. It is also difficult to ensure that the answers are recorded properly.

Forms Management

During the research phase, the procedures analyst should decide if new forms are needed, if old forms are to be revised, or if the current forms are adequate. Even if the procedures analyst does not control the forms function in the organization, he should sit down with the major users to understand the purpose and consequences of the new or revised forms. If a current form is used or can be used in a proposed policy or procedure, the procedures analyst should reanalyze the form in the same manner as for a new form. The procedures analyst will find that the same kinds of questions asked of individuals for procedures will also apply to questions about forms. In many cases, the sequence of the form will direct the sequence of the process, policy, or procedure. When the policy or procedure is written in advance of forms, there is a tendency to make the policy or procedure fit the form — and this does not always work!

Conversion of Selected Alternate Solution
to Writing Format

Once an alternate has been selected and the process and procedures are defined, the procedures analyst can begin the process of converting the relevant information to the standard format presented in Chapter 4. This format has been designed so that the procedures analyst can insert information in a logical sequence. As you will see, the main place for the process flow of the procedure falls within the seventh heading of the writing format, or the "Procedures Section." This is the **TIE** from the research phase to the draft of the policy or procedure.

With the procedures analyst turning to writing the rough draft, the cross-functional should not be disbanded yet. The team will still be needed to help review the comments to the rough draft while its going through the user and management review groups. The team is especially crucial to the successful implementation and training of the policy or procedure. While there may be an idle period while the draft is being prepared, the procedures analyst should keep the team informed as to his progress. The better the communication, the better the chance that the policy or procedure will be well received by those who use it.

Special Skills Required: Speaking and Listening

The procedures analyst needs strong speaking and listening skills. These skills will help to strengthen the relationship with the users. Although the procedures analyst will spend most of his research time listening, there are certain pitfalls he should be aware of when speaking to others. As a speaker, some common practices to avoid are listed below:

1. Using vague or unfamiliar terms;
2. Giving too much or too little information;
3. Exhibiting nonverbal behavior that conflicts with a verbal message;
4. Failing to respect basic human rights; and
5. Creating defensive attitudes within listeners.

Perhaps the biggest problem is avoiding creating defensive attitudes within listeners. The procedures analyst needs to protect against appearing to be a "know-it-all" or acting superior to the listener. When confronted by such behavior, the listener may become defensive and refuse to be frank and honest with the procedures analyst.

Listening Skills

Good listening skills are fundamental to the procedures analyst's effectiveness. The two main characteristics of good listening are thinking and concentrating. Both are influenced by factors such as personal background, age, intelligence, motivation, emotion, ability to detect ideas, memory, vocabulary, handling of distractions effectively, and the evaluation of messages received. Listening is as automatic as breathing. Retaining what has been heard, however, is very difficult. To be a good listener, certain bad habits should be avoided:

1. Faking attention;
2. Premature dismissal of a subject that seems uninteresting;
3. Criticizing the delivery and physical appearance of the speaker; and
4. Yielding to distractions such as the closing of a door, the closing of a window, someone chewing gum, or daydreaming;

To overcome these bad habits, the procedures analyst should become conscious of his listening habits and strive for the following habits:

1. Take time to listen and not let the mind stray;
2. Show acknowledgment to speaker that he is listening;
3. Reflect or paraphrase the message back to the speaker; this practice is to let the speaker know if message is being understood;
4. Ensure facial and body movement agree with the listening habits; and
5. Never evaluate while someone is speaking; if the procedures analyst should evaluate early, he may fail to hear the rest of the message.

Although most people would like to believe that they have good listening habits, studies have shown that listening is a concentrated effort and that most people retain only about 25 percent of what they hear. Even if the procedures analyst thinks he is already an excellent listener, it cannot hurt to take at least one course dealing with listening skills.

Note Taking

The purpose of note taking is to summarize and to record the information that is extracted during the research stage. The ability to take notes while listening is a skill that should be learned. It is important that the procedures analyst use a note taking system that does not detract from listening. If note taking is done efficiently, it is almost certain to improve the procedures analyst's attentiveness.

If the procedures analyst is consciously aware of how he takes notes, the method of note taking can be improved. He should attempt to capture the basic ideas presented on paper. Writing complete sentences is desirable but not always necessary. The use of abbreviations, underscoring, arrows, stars, or numbers can be helpful when taking "quick" notes.

The most common method of note taking is the outline form. It provides structure to writing and assures that there is a beginning, a middle, and an ending. Outlining makes large or complex subjects easier to handle by breaking them into manageable parts. While outlining is an excellent note taking tool, the procedures analyst should also consider documenting the process using a *flow chart*. It is your choice as to which method you want to use for note taking.

Using Flow Charts
as a Note Taking Method

In most of the research required for a proposed policy or procedure, the interrelationships are difficult to keep clearly in mind without some visual representation. It is recommended that a *flow chart* be used for organizing thoughts, in addition to using a word processing table or some other method for outlining the steps of a policy or procedure. The flow chart is a graphic presentation of a procedure. It is composed of a series of actions and decisions framed in boxes and linked by arrows. The basic parts of a flow chart are action boxes and decision boxes, start and stop boxes, loop decision boxes, and connectors. However, it would be acceptable to use just rectangle "action" boxes to describe all events.

The flow chart is especially useful to the procedures analyst for analyzing the logic necessary in a proposed policy or procedure. It helps lead the procedures analyst through the correct sequence of events from start to finish. A method for creating and using flow charts is detailed in my third book, "Achieving 100% Compliance of Policies and Procedures."

Summary

The major emphasis of this chapter has been the identification of core business processes and the content needed for a system of policies and procedures. Research methods have been presented for identifying alternate solutions and then searching out the details of that selected process. These included: (1) identification of core business processes; (2) business process reengineering; (3) benchmarking; (4) networking; (5) obtaining ideas from forms management; (6) obtaining ideas and information from external certifications and regulations; (7) cross-functional teams; (8) employing meeting techniques such as brainstorming, networking, interviewing, or questionnaires; and (9) proper listening, speaking, and note taking skills.

With the selection of the alternative and the mutual agreement from the cross-functional team, the procedures analyst can turn to the writing format in Chapter 4 to begin populating the rough draft. The remaining chapters will be devoted to completing the rough draft, obtaining approval, distributing and implementing the draft and training employees in the use of the policy or procedure.

Refer to my three other policy and procedure books (see below) to provide added detail in finding content, writing policies and procedures, aligning content with vision and the strategic direction of the organization, building a cross-functional team, and finding an effective solution.

1. "Best Practices in Policies and Procedures"
2. "Achieving 100% Compliance of Policies and Procedures"
3. "7 Steps to Better Written Policies and Procedures"

Chapter 3

FORMS MANAGEMENT

Vital Importance of Forms Control

Put simply, forms are critical to the operations of an organization. They play a vital role in business systems development. When it comes to the use of forms, many people will follow what the forms say rather than the written procedures. Hence, there is a close link between forms control and procedures' analysis. Forms management is not just involved with the elimination of paperwork. It also creates forms used by organizations to conduct business efficiently.

Since policies and procedures are normally written with the intention of improving a situation, it seems logical that the forms related to that business process should be carefully analyzed and designed by the same people doing the procedures' analysis and publication. An inadequate analysis of either the procedures' or the forms' system could lead to an incomplete solution and possibly misdirect the procedures analyst.

Forms' and Procedures' Analysts Working Together

There is a close relationship between the forms' and procedures' system. Clearly these two analysts perform similar functions. In small companies, often the procedures analyst is also the forms analyst. In larger companies, the two analysts often work side-by-side in the same department or as peers on cross-functional teams. The importance of these two positions being close to one another cannot be emphasized enough. I have seen countless examples where procedures cannot be designed without first examining the forms' system. Whenever I begin work on a business process, my first step is to analyze and design the necessary forms for the business process. Very often, the work done in forms analysis and design leads you to the correct solution for the procedures' system. If the form is analyzed correctly according to form industry standards, then usually the basic flow of the procedure has already been defined. If the form has been being laid out in a logical order for easy fill-in, then the flow of the procedure will normally follow these steps. As you will see in Chapter 4, the most important section of a Procedure is the "Procedures Section" (Heading 7.0) in the writing format. Typically, the procedure is presented from start to end in this section. This is how a well-designed form should be laid out. This is the reason it is so important for the procedures analyst to learn and understand the role of the forms' analyst.

I have also found it most useful to show an actual sample of the most current form at the back of the procedure as an appendix or figure. There are advantages and disadvantages to this practice. It becomes your choice about which way you want to handle forms in your procedures. The main advantage is that the reader can see the form (s) with the procedure in one place. Often, if the readers have to reference a form in a different location, they will not bother. This could cause the wrong form to be used and lead to all kinds of problems in the business process. The main disadvantage is that each time the form changes, the procedure has to be revised, published, and distributed just to reflect the form changes. This can be wasteful depending on the number of procedures in circulation and the size of the company.

As for me, I believe in being thorough so I include a copy of any related form in each procedure that I write and publish. I might note that in each company for which I have worked, I have been both the forms manager and the procedures manager. The relationship is too important to leave the two functions separate. I think you can appreciate the problems that could arise if forms are designed without procedures being involved or if procedures are developed and published without forms being involved. The most important problem is one of credibility. It can be very frustrating to users of a system not to be able to access a new, or revised, form that has been referenced in a policy or procedure. Users will use the old form and make the same mistakes that the new form is trying to correct. They may not use the guidelines of the new policy or procedure either. This causes an element of confusion for the user.

Forms Explained

Business forms are management tools that help the writing, transmission, and reporting of business information. There are two ways to view a form: printed and electronic. A printed paper form is "a document bearing instructions with repetitive information preprinted in a fixed position to save writing and reference time." An electronic form is "a document stored on an electronic memory device that is made available on a computer monitor when needed."

Forms are efficient business tools and are here to stay. Prophecies of paperless offices have not materialized. The volume of business data being transmitted by electronic communications has dramatically increased. However, millions of paper forms are still used to initiate and process business transactions. Forms are used in every office and will continue to be used in the future. Forms ask the proper questions in an organized manner. They provide the proper space for fill-in information.

If there were no business forms, many instructions and communications would have to be given verbally or through notes. Information would be overlooked because there would be no organized checklist of information. Time would be wasted in organizing thoughts. The lack of documented communications could end in chaos, inconsistent decisions, and legal matters.

Forms Can Reveal Much About an Organization

Forms can tell your customers a great deal about your organization. For example, appearance alone can imply that you are either old-fashioned or progressive. Ease of completion may mean the difference between renewed business and the client going elsewhere. In industries like insurance and banking, this can be an important issue. As forms are frequently the lifeblood of the organization, a good forms management department may mean the difference in your whole organization's vision and mission statements. I recall seeing a "Visitor's" form in the corporate office of a major film company that was crudely created on a typewriter. This form projected a poor image of the company. Image is everything for some companies. This image can be enhanced through a well-developed forms management program and a system of policies and procedures.

Objectives of Forms Management

Forms management is a program devoted to *controlling forms in the organization*. It consists of three basic functions: control, design, and analysis. The main objectives of forms management are to:

1. Provide efficient forms at the lowest possible printing and processing costs, consistent with the form's role in the information system; and

2. Produce attractive, effective forms that will enhance the organization's image, consistent with economical procurement considerations.

The goals of forms management are to reduce the number of form types, reduce the number of actual forms in use, reduce the number of errors, produce more efficient business systems, develop form design standards and guidelines, and extend the use of well-conceived and proven forms.

Forms Evaluation Starts With Analysis

Forms management begins with the analysis of the form. It results in an image on paper or in the computer. The first step in forms analysis is to decide if the form is necessary. If so, then it is further decided what data it should contain, what type of form it should be, and how it should be designed. This is forms analysis. It should not be confused with forms design or the arrangement of data on a form.

Forms analysis defines the purpose of the system, explores present forms and methods, and exposes all of the costs associated with the present system. Proper system analysis decides how each piece of paper relates to the company's information system, how each form is used, and most important, why the form is necessary. Before the analysis is complete, every part of every form should prove its worth to the system. New forms may be required, but their necessity should be shown.

The forms analyst will do basic fact-finding. The form will be challenged. Its sponsor will be interviewed. Forms will be analyzed for common or repetitive data to eliminate the costs of duplication or errors through creative design. Successful forms analysis can eliminate unnecessary forms, combine similar forms, justify new and/or improved forms, change the sequence of forms distribution for greater understanding, or simplify form items for greater clarity.

When analyzing the forms system, the procedures analyst should make a mental note of existing policies and procedures that may need changing if a form is created or revised. Additionally, the procedures analyst can recommend to management new policies and procedures that should be written explaining either new, or current forms that have never been included in a policy or a procedure.

Forms Design Follows Analysis

Forms design is the creation of the layout of the items and features of a form. It determines how the information on the form can be arranged and displayed in the best manner. This idea of forms design is basically the same for paper and electronic forms. Good forms design should:

1. Be easy to read and understand;
2. Be easy to complete or fill in;
3. Be easy to use or process;
4. Allow data to be easily retrieved;
5. Reduce the chance of error; and
6. Create a favorable mental attitude.

The forms designer should understand that a form is an information systems tool. The value of a form is the efficiency with which it communicates in the information system. The users are the final judges of whether a form is functional. A form will be used correctly only if it is designed to meet the needs of everyone who should read, write, audit, or file it. Without buy-in of the people involved, the new business process, procedure, or form is doomed to failure.

Printing and Using the Form

The next step is to determine how the design will be converted to camera-ready art. *Camera-ready art* refers to the final layout, paper or electronic, that is ready to be printed or used electronically. If the form is to be used in a paper format, then it needs to be reproduced. There are several printing options including the traditional forms manufacturer, speedy copy retailer, or an in-house print shop or printing equipment. The electronic form is generally introduced to the company through an email notification. While copies of an electronic form may be printed somewhere in the process, the form is generally not printed at the onset.

With the form available in stock, the form can now be incorporated into the policies and procedures system. I have found that if you are good at analyzing and designing a form you can have full confidence in printing the form EVEN before the analysis of the relevant business process is completed. This can be a real time saving step because it is very important that all forms referenced in a business process be available when the final policy or procedure is published. You can easily lose credibility by referencing a form in a policy or procedure that is not available.

Electronic Forms

With current technology, it has become possible to integrate electronic forms with an on-line policies and procedures manual. The first rule of an electronic forms system is that it should emulate the paper system in every positive way. A company should not even consider an electronic forms management system until it has developed a successful manual forms management system. This is a mistake often made by companies that think technology is the key to their problems. Key benefits of electronic forms management include revision control, database lookup, automatic defaults, automatic help, calculations, data stamping, digital signatures, reporting, and email.

Converting from paper to electronic forms can reduce the costs of printing, storing, managing, fill in and distributing forms. This is achieved through increased productivity, saving time, gaining office and warehouse space, and saving money previously lost in destroying forms that required revisions, or became obsolete. Unlike traditional forms, electronic forms systems not only create forms but they also manage and process them. Electronic forms can be text-based or graphics based. Like procedures, an electronic version of a form can have many advantages. With electronic forms, we can now be assured that the form being used is the correct version and that anyone in the organization can find it easily and quickly.

With the rapid expansion of technology, electronic form capabilities are being added to a variety of on-line sources including the on-line manual and Intranets (Internet-like networks used internally in an organization) and Extranets (an Intranet that's open to outside access by selective partners). This presents multiple problems that are not the subject of this book. For more information on electronic forms, I suggest you contact your local forms association for information and references.

While it is understandable that management wants to save costs, reduce paper, cut back on printing and limit the number of stored forms, care should be taken to ensure that all of the pitfalls and bugs are worked out before implementation. When this technology was first introduced, companies were very excited about the prospects of replacing all paper forms. Some years later these same organizations were facing the realization that electronic forms conversion could be very expensive.

> Without careful planning, electronic forms can cost more than the paper they are designed to replace.

My advice is to go slowly; and seek the advice of the form professionals dedicated to electronic form systems. Seek out professional forms associations for assistance and direction.

Learning More About Forms Management

As the subject of this book is developing policies and procedures and not the development of a forms management department, I will refer you to my fellow forms professionals for this task. There are several sources for you to pursue. I will start you in the right direction but then it is your choice to pursue some of these avenues to improve the quality of your policies and procedures system. Start with the Business Forms Management Association (BFMA) website (http://www.bfma.org/) as it contains good ideas and links to other forms' websites.

Summary

Forms management plays an important role in a company's operations. Forms provide an efficient and economical way to write instructions and to control actions in business. Without forms, a business would be unable to function. Nearly all business activities are initiated and controlled by paperwork. The efficiency of these activities is, in turn, dependent on the efficiency of the forms within the paperwork system, and this system is a necessary component of all business systems.

Both the procedures analyst and the forms analyst are interested in forms systems. Whenever a form is designed and/or revised, some policy or procedure will be affected. When policies and procedures, on the other hand, are suggested, the problem or the situation for which they are being developed usually affects a form system either directly or indirectly. Consequently, when a new or revised form is created or changed, the forms analyst should inform the procedures analyst. Similarly, when there is a new, or revised policy or procedure, the forms analyst should be informed.

The information in this chapter should provide both the forms and the procedures analyst a good starting point. It is their choice as to how much they want to learn about their respective disciplines to further their credibility and reputation.

Chapter 4

WRITING FORMAT

Reasons for a Writing Format

The writing format is the heart of a policies and procedures system. It provides a structure for information collected during the research phase. A logical, structured format is a basic requirement for any policy or procedure. Coherence is developed by a smooth flow of thought and by the logical flow of information. It can be very frustrating to a reader if the information is not clearly presented in a logical order from one procedure to the next. It is common to find policies and procedures written with few, or no headings, or with headings that change from procedure to procedure. This kind of inconsistency can make it difficult to read a policy or procedure. For example, if a procedure is written in a different format each time, the reader does not know what to expect. I have seen policies and procedures written in outline form one time and in paragraph form the next. The reader does not know what to expect and it can be confusing.

Most readers need to find information quickly. Research suggests that the way many documents are written inhibits easy reading. Many documents do not support fast reading because major ideas are buried, headings are ambiguous or uninformative to the reader, important detail is hard to locate, and instructions are either nonexistent or difficult to find or understand. Consistency saves readers time because they can find the information they need quickly and focus on content rather than format. A specific writing format is recommended in each of my four books on policies and procedures. The writing format is the heart of any policy and procedure system. Without a standard method of writing, policies and procedures tend to be inconsistent, inaccurate, and inefficient.

Recommended Writing Format

The writing format recommended in this book is called the *Basic Writing Format*. For policies and procedures, the structure remains the same, only the content changes. This writing format enables the reader to understand the main objectives, ideas, methods, or processes being presented in the first several pages of a document. Sometimes the reader may not have to read any further. My writing format is perhaps the easiest method available for readers who want to skim a document. The reason behind this claim resides in the fact that the reader can understand the basis of the entire policy or procedure within the first several pages of the document. This format is also neatly laid out. This is a benefit to the reader because he's more inclined to read something that appears structured and orderly than something that appears unstructured and disorganized.

Playscript Writing Format:
Technical Instructions Only

While there are several types of writing formats suggested by different authors, all but one generally focus on the similar type of sections for the format. The exception to this rule is called the *Playscript Writing Format*. Being a systems person, I personally prefer the basic writing format for writing policies and procedures. However, the *Playscript Writing Format* does have merit for writing technical instructions, or step-by-step instructions for carrying out a specific task.

The *Playscript Writing Format* gives you a step-by-step flow of the work from start to finish. A key point about the *Playscript Writing Format* is that it only applies to the procedural content of a manual (Section 7.0 of the *Basic Writing Format*). This is why it could be used for technical instructions such as explaining how to write a purchase requisition or how to turn a computer on and start a program.

When writing policies and procedures, it is my preference that you give the reader all the information needed to read and understand what is being presented. This is what the *Basic Writing Format* does. The *Playscript Writing Format* provides step-by-step instructions of a person's role, a step number, and the action. It does not explain the details nor does it tell you the purpose of the technical instructions.

As Playscript is not the subject of this book, I have included an excellent reference in the bibliography written by a world renowned author and speaker, Robert Barnett. Other books may be located by through an extensive library and Internet search. I have included an example of the *Playscript Writing Format* in Appendix C.

Basic Writing Format

There are seven principal headings to the basic writing format. The information that goes into a heading will be called a *section*. As you start to understand the purpose of each section, you will realize how easy it is to insert information into each section as the information is gathered during the research phase. Typically, most of the information can be collected in this way and the task of writing the policy or procedure draft is greatly reduced by the time when the research phase is completed. I think you will find this is a major advantage to using the Basic Writing Format.

I have been using this writing format for the past 28 years and except for the numbering scheme, there have been few changes in the heading titles and hierarchical structure. I started with six headings and have recently added a seventh heading to accommodate a revision history. It is good practice to incorporate a revision history into any document that could change. When I do research and work with cross-functional teams, I often bring this writing format with me to the meetings and we work on one section at a time.

Seven Principal Headings

The seven headings will always appear in the sequence presented below for both policies or procedures. There are ONLY seven headings and each heading is always the same except for the third heading that will be explained later.

Each heading begins with a number. The heading could be highlighted with underscoring, bold type, or capitals. It is your choice as to writing style. In my examples, I will underscore the words. In printed manuals, underscoring is acceptable but in on-line manuals or on the Internet, underscoring typically means that the information is linked to something else. Thus, the use of bolding or capital letters may be a better choice.

Seven Principal Headings

1.0	Purpose
2.0	Revision History
3.0	Persons Affected
4.0	Policy
5.0	Definitions
6.0	Responsibilities
7.0	Procedures

Depending on whether you are writing a policy or procedure, the content that goes into each section will vary. If a heading is not used, or if there is no content, then the words, "Not Applicable" are written under the appropriate section heading. It is not acceptable to eliminate the heading. If you remember to always list seven headings, you will not face this inconsistency factor.

> **Each of the seven headings is required for <u>every</u> policy or procedure regardless of content.**

I will stress this point one more time, always include seven headings, regardless of the content. The reader is looking for the same headings each time. If you change your headings from one policy or procedure to the next, the reader will wonder if you left something out.

While there is only one *Basic Writing Format*, the content of the policy and the procedure will differ slightly. The term, "Required," means that information should be written for this section. The term, "Optional," means that information could be written for this section but more than likely, it will be blank. In this case, the words, "Not Applicable," could be used. The terms, "Required" and "Optional" have nothing to do with the headings, and the original seven headings are still required. For example, when preparing a rough draft, it would be a format mistake to include the terms, "Required" and "Optional" after each heading.

Policy Writing Format

1.0	Purpose *(Required)*
2.0	Revision History *(Required)*
3.0	Persons Affected *(Required)*
4.0	Policy *(Required)*
5.0	Definitions *(Optional)*
6.0	Responsibilities *(Optional)*
7.0	Procedures *(Optional)*

Procedure Writing Format

1.0	Purpose *(Required)*
2.0	Revision History *(Required)*
3.0	Persons Affected *(Required)*
4.0	Policy *(Required)*
5.0	Definitions *(Required)*
6.0	Responsibilities *(Required)*
7.0	Procedures *(Required)*

Numbering of Headings

Each of the seven headings should be assigned a consecutive number. There are three common numbering systems: Roman numerals, Arabic numbering, and decimal numbers. All are acceptable. It is your choice.

Within each system, you can indent to another number or letter. There should be at least two indents within each heading to keep within correct grammatical rules. I do want to add that it is possible to use these numbering systems without indenting. I personally do not like this technique because I find it hard to read. Again, it is your choice. Refer to the two sample procedures in the Appendices D and E. I have used the decimal system with indented and without indented numbering.

Using the Seven Headings

The use of each of the seven headings will be discussed and examples given for each. These examples are not necessarily related. I am just providing sample wording to give you a sense of the writing style I use. I will give examples of each heading in the following several pages. Refer to Appendices D, E, and H for samples of these headings.

1.0 Purpose

This is the first heading of the *Writing Format*. The *Purpose* section explains the objective(s) for writing the policy or procedure. When writing purpose statements, you might want to consider using a consistent opening phrase. The purpose normally contains two or three sentences. It should be comprehensive and concise in its meaning. Abbreviations or acronyms should not be used, if they have not been explained yet. This is often a mistake when deciding the title of a policy or procedure. Examples include:

A. This procedure establishes guidelines by which employees may discuss grievances with management.

B. This policy establishes the company's position on Equal Opportunity and Affirmative Action Programs.

C. This procedure establishes guidelines by which employees are paid for and reimbursed for expenses incurred while traveling on business.

A consistent opening phrase is, "This procedure establishes . . . "

50

2.0 Revision History

This heading shows revisions to a policy or procedure. It provides a history to the document. This is an important section for ISO 9000 Quality Standards and to the CMM as it is a requirement of those standards. A revision history shows the date of the change, the revision number, and the modification. The original document is always 1.0.

Date	Rev. No.	Modification
01/02/02	1.0	New document
06/05/02	1.1	New form

3.0 Persons Affected

This heading identifies the users of a policy or procedure. This is the only heading that may change its wording. It could be titled, "Areas Affected," "Departments Affected," "Customers Affected," and so on. It can also be a combination of choices such as "All Employees and Customers Affected." Examples include:

A. All employees of (name of organization or department).
B. All domestic divisions of (name of organization).
C. This policy applies only to the Marketing and Purchasing departments.

4.0 Policy

This is the MOST IMPORTANT HEADING for the policy or procedure. It provides the general organizational attitude of the company, as well as reflecting the basic objectives, goals, or vision of the organization. Even if you decided in Chapter 1 to write a separate policy manual, this section heading is still required. In this case, it could be an abbreviated version of the policy.

It has been my experience that the inclusion of a policy statement within a procedure makes the procedure easier to understand and shows the company's strategy. If the policy statement were in another reference document, then the reader would have to go find another document before he could understand the true intent of this document. This is **a very important point** and is worth repeating. The whole purpose of writing an easily read and understood policy or procedure is for the reader to understand and retain the information on the first reading of the material. If the reader should reference another document in another manual, it takes time and effort, and more than likely, it will not happen. The reader will be using procedural information without the whole story. I know from experience that it is cumbersome to have to seek out another document just to be able to understand this one you are reading. Examples include:

A. It is the policy of (name of organization) to reimburse employees for all expenses incurred while on company business.
B. It is the policy of (name of organization) to:
    1). Prohibit the sale of personal items during working hours.
    2). Ensure personal items are not ordered and received through the Receiving Department.
    3). Provide bulletin board space for employees to advertise personal items to sell.
    4). Provide annual bazaar days to employees who wish to sell their personal items or other handicrafts.

As with the purpose statement, it is preferred to start the policy statement with words that are consistent from document to document. The words, "It is the policy of . . . " let the reader know immediately that is the policy statement for the policy or procedure. If only one objective is being expressed, then the policy statement does not need to be broken into subdivisions. If there is more than one objective, then subdividing the heading is recommended.

Using Policy Statement Heading Instead of
a Policy Manual - A Personal Example

When I first started using the policy heading for policies and procedures, I was in the practice of writing separate policy documents and placing them alongside procedures. The only difference was the color of the paper.

52

I used blue paper for the policies and white paper for the procedures to make them easier to identify. More recently, I have eliminated the use of a separate policy document. I have incorporated the essence of the policy into the *Policy* section of the *Writing Format*. This is a simple solution to a problem faced by procedures analysts for decades.

For years, companies usually created two manuals, one for policies and the other for procedures. They were kept side-by-side and each had their own format, content, and distribution. Typically, the policy would be the guiding force for the procedures and generally there was a direct link between a policy and several procedures. I found this practice difficult for readers to both access and understand. While many companies still continue this practice today, I do not. I use the policy heading within the procedure document, thus eliminating the need for policy documents or separate manuals.

For ISO 9000 Quality Standards, there is typically a manual for policies, a manual for procedures, and a manual for technical work instructions. It is because of these situations that I am presenting information you will need to write a separate manual for policies and one for procedures.

5.0 Definitions

This heading is important for all procedures. It is normally not necessary in a policy. For a policy, the words, "Not Applicable," are written under this heading. This is the heading where the procedures analyst will define abbreviations, acronyms, forms, words infrequently used, and technical terms. Anything that might not be understood through a casual reading should be included in this section.

A definition is *an explanation of an object or idea that distinguishes it from all other objects or ideas*. A definition could be an explanation of what is included and what is excluded. Examples of definitions include:

1. COD - Collect on Delivery. This term is often confused with "Cash on Delivery." It means to collect cash or a check.
2. Union - A continuing, long-term association of employees, formed for the specific purpose of advancing and protecting the interests of members of their working relationships.

3. Receiving Report (Form No.) - Six-part form used to record the receipt of goods into the company. (See Exhibit II.)
4. ISO - International Standards Organization.

Defining forms is just as important as defining technical terms. All forms referred to in a policy or procedure should be clearly described in the *Definitions* section. Any information pertinent to the form should be included in the definition along with an indication as to where to find a current sample of the form. It has been my personal preference to show a copy of the form as an appendix to the policy or the procedure. Others will refer the reader to a forms catalogue or to Stationery Stores or Forms Control for the form. While it poses an extra effort to include current forms in the document, it eliminates the possibility of the person using the wrong form. If the reader should go to another source to find a document referenced, it is unlikely to happen.

The instructions for completing the form should be an integral part of the appropriate exhibit rather than being contained in the body of the procedure, unless the main point of the procedure is the form. Instructions can normally be eliminated if the form has been designed to be self-instructing. This is the trend of forms design. Since form instructions are a part of the procedures document, this is another reason the procedures analyst needs to completely understand the role of the forms analyst.

6.0 Responsibilities

This heading is required in procedures but is normally not necessary in a policy. For a policy, the words, "Not Applicable," should be written under this heading. The *Responsibilities* section is a short summary of the duties of the person(s) involved with the procedure. This section should be written in the same sequence of events that occurs under the *Procedures* section. Often the procedures analyst should write the procedures section BEFORE the *Responsibilities* section. It is important to stress that the *Responsibilities* section is written in the same sequence of events as outlined under the *Procedures* section.

By the time the reader has read this section, he should have a fairly good grasp of the intention behind the procedure. It is at this point that the reader may choose not to read any further if he is not directly affected by the implementation of the procedure. Examples include:

A. The requester shall complete the check request form, no. 101.
B. The controller shall approve all check request forms.
C. The Accounts Payable supervisor shall generate the check after receiving an approved check request form.
D. The vice president of Finance shall sign the check before it is returned to the requester.

7.0 <u>Procedures</u>

This heading is required for all procedures but it is not normally necessary in a policy. For a policy, the words, "Not Applicable" should be written in this section. The *Procedures* section defines and outlines the rules, regulations, methods, timing, place, and personnel responsible for accomplishing the policy as stated under the *Policy* heading. This section is where the procedures analyst outlines the step-by-step process from start to finish. This is the section that is equivalent to an entire procedure written in the *Playscript* format.

The *Procedures* section provides a direct link to the process identified during the research phase. Most of the time spent during research is often spent defining a new, or revised, business process. The first six sections of the *Basic Writing Format* can often be defined, or filled in, following the research phase from the material collected during the cross-functional team meetings. The example below is a shortened procedure for processing a book request.

1. When an employee finds a book he thinks will be useful on his job, he will complete a check request form and submit it to his supervisor for approval.

    a. If the supervisor concurs that the book is business-related, then he signs and dates the check request form.

    b. The supervisor submits the check request form to Accounting for approval and processing.

2. If the check request form has been completed according to the form instructions contained in this procedure, the controller will sign and date the form, showing approval.

    a. The approved check request form is given to the supervisor of Accounting, who in turn generates a check.

    b. The check is returned to the controller for signing.

3. The controller returns the signed check to the supervisor of Accounting, who in turn sends the check to the requester for payment of the book.

Sometimes it may seem as if the *Procedures* section is a repetition of the *Responsibilities* section. The writing format has been structured such that the first six headings provide an overview of the policy or the procedure. The seventh heading provides the details necessary to accomplish the activities as set forth in the *Policy* statement.

Optional Headings

There are no optional sections. I make this point because this may be causing confusion among some of those who have adopted my style of writing policies and procedures. To maintain consistency from document to document, I have elected not to add an eighth or ninth heading. It would not be consistent and could add confusion for the reader.

Exhibits, Figures, and Flow Charts

There is no established format for exhibits or figures since there are many possible formats. When designing an exhibit or figure, the procedures analyst should try to maintain consistency in fonts, typefaces, margins, and page numbers. I have used a flow chart hundreds of times to help me in developing the possibilities and contingencies of a process. It is a useful tool to illustrate the possible branches of a process. However, I do not recommend that a copy of the flow chart be incorporated into the procedures document. Using a flow chart may be useful to the procedures analyst but more often than not, the reader skips over it. Thus, it is from my personal experience that a flow chart should not be a figure or exhibit within the procedure. It could be used during training or implementation BUT NOT as an aid to the reader in a procedures document.

Printing (or Copying) Policies and Procedures

There are several ways to print policies and procedures. It is your choice and perhaps a decision from senior management. Most often policies and procedures reproduced on photocopiers, unless the distribution is large, is too expensive to print at a retail printer. This choice should not make a difference even if preprinted forms are used or if a paper color is selected for a policy or a procedure.

Approval Signatures

The location of signatures on a policy or procedure document can be either on the first page, last page, or on a separate page. I prefer signatures on the first page because then it leaves little doubt as to the authority of the published document. If your management agrees that the approval signatures will be placed on the first page, the signatures can only go on the top or the bottom. The bottom is a more logical location unless you are using a printed form. This way you can design a special location closer to the top for approval signatures.

If your management agrees that the approval signatures will be placed on the last page of the document, the signatures can be placed approximately two inches below the last text of the policy or procedure. The location of the approval page could be referenced in the table of contents of the policy or procedure.

I do not recommend the last page for several reasons. First, the last page of text may not be the last page of the procedure if you have included exhibits or appendices making the approval signatures hard to find. Second, if the reader does not read the entire procedure, he will not know who approved the document and may not respect its authority.

If your management wants a separate sheet of approval signatures, then it could be placed in front of the first page of the policy or procedure document. While this is a visible place for signatures, it covers up the first page of the policy or procedure and can have the effect of deterring someone from reading the actual document.

Policy and Procedure Numbers

The numbering system for policies and procedures should be easy and straightforward. The numbers should be sequentially assigned, starting with an even number such as 100 or 1000. If needed, provisions could be made to assign a predetermined range of numbers to specific areas, although this practice has its disadvantages. It takes careful planning to avoid running out of numbers. For example, if you have three departments, the numbering series could be set up as follows:

1000-1100 Administrative Services
1100-2000 Accounting and Finance
2000-2999 Manufacturing

If you assign all of the numbers for the Administrative Services area, and a new policy or procedure needs to be written, then this sequence cannot be used. It becomes a serious problem to change a numbering scheme or to alter the manuals to reflect a change in numbering. This is one of the reasons that I prefer a random numbering system.

Summary

The *Basic Writing Format* presented in this chapter will enable the procedures analyst to organize information collected during research efficiently and quickly. The structure of the format leaves nothing to the imagination. When the procedures analyst first uses the writing format, difficulties will be experienced, but the procedures analyst should quickly realize its potential. The method of gathering "like" information for seven sections is very simple to learn and apply. The headings make it easy to place "like" items together and to exclude unrelated items from inappropriate sections. The procedures analyst should not be too concerned if he chooses the format for a policy when the format for a procedure should have been selected. The intention and the effects are the same to the reader, despite the writing format used.

The *Playscript Writing Format* has been suggested as a writing format for technical instructions where general information is not required for management, audits, or historical reasons. This format is used for writing technical instructions, creating desk or office routines, or for form instructions.

The third book in my series about policies and procedures, "7 Steps to Better Written Policies and Procedures" is written entirely on the writing format. Checklists, guidelines, and exercises are provided to help you write better. This third book is an excellent companion for this book. It provides extensive information on each section of the writing format including the right way and the wrong way to develop the content for each section.

Chapter 5

WRITING STYLE

Effective Writing

For communication to be effective, writers need empathy, or the ability to place themselves in the shoes of the readers and understand how the readers will view the writing. It is difficult to test every policy or procedure before it is implemented. Thus, the procedures analyst needs to take care to write as clearly as possible based on the information gathered during the research phase.

As a prerequisite to good writing, the procedures analyst should try to be familiar with the rules of English usage, spelling, vocabulary, punctuation, grammar, sentence and paragraph structure, proofreading, and editing. A knowledge of words, phrases, clauses, basic structures, modification, and agreement is essential to good writing, but such knowledge does not guarantee that your rough drafts will be written well. He should think logically, organize ideas, write clearly, concisely, tactfully, and courteously.

Organization of Thoughts

The procedures analyst should have the ability to organize ideas from his research into a logical plan. The reader needs to read information that is easy to retain for later application. Not only should the information be organized into a logical plan from the beginning to the end of a policy or procedure, but each sentence within each paragraph, and each paragraph within each heading, should be organized as well.

One successful method of defining the organizational process in writing involves (1) dividing the subject into its component parts; (2)

analyzing these parts in a systematic order; (3) developing each part and (4) providing the connective tissue to draw all parts and details into a logical order. This is the ultimate purpose of the *Basic Writing Format* presented in Chapter 4.

Writing Clarity

The procedures analyst should aim to be as clear as possible and to make every sentence mean exactly what it is intended. It should also be incapable of misinterpretation. For example, it may be the policy of a company to provide "three weeks of paid vacation time each year." It is unclear if the employee receives the full three weeks at the beginning or the end of the year, or if he accrues the vacation during the year. Consequently, the sentence is not clear and the stated policy will be subject to varying interpretations by employees.

If a message is to be clear, it should contain correct and complete information expressed concisely. A person may write something that is clear in meaning without being accurate. For example, a procedure may say that "it takes one week to process a purchase requisition," whereas, in reality the process only takes three days. This problem could be avoided by not specifying the processing time or by specifying a deadline time such as, "the purchase requisition will be processed within six working days."

The chances that a message will be clear are greatly improved if the procedures analyst uses short, simple, familiar words; constructs correct and logical sentences and paragraphs; maintains a level of readability appropriate to the readers; and uses examples and exhibits to illustrate points. The main task is to create an image in the reader's mind that is the same image as perceived by the procedures analyst.

Word Meanings

Procedure manuals should be written with the simplest words possible while still conveying a meaning to the reader. A major problem with technical manuals is that the writer aims at correctness and chooses the biggest and most specific words. While I am not against the use of dictionaries, words serve little useful purpose if they cannot be understood. Correctness should not be an end in itself. Manuals should not be written like college textbooks requiring exhaustive study. People in a work environment do not have time to study. Work place manuals should not require the reader to have an open dictionary or thesaurus on his desk.

Jargon

Jargon is a part of everyday life. While almost every individual group of people has its own language, or jargon, it should be avoided if there is even the slightest indication that it will not be understood. If a word is common for an audience for which the manual is intended, then it is appropriate. If jargon is used, the procedures analyst should make it a point to define those terms in the *Definitions* section of the *Basic Writing Format*.

If the readers are primarily engineers, then the use of scientific language may be welcomed. Whereas if office personnel are the readers, technical language may be annoying due to a lack of familiarity with the specialized terms. One of the most common faults in today's business communication is the use of computer jargon. This is particularly prevalent in manuals written by computer system analysts.

Spelling, Abbreviations, and Punctuation

For effective communication, the procedures analyst should follow the preferred usage for spelling, capitalization, and punctuation. General guidelines can be found in the reference section of most dictionaries. Uniform spelling is essential. Spelling is a convenient test of literacy and even of respectability. Careless spelling mistakes should be avoided. For example, *a lot* should be *a lot*; *inturn* should be *in turn*; *alright* should be *all right*; *recieving* should be *receiving*, and so on. In today's technology, most word processing software is equipped with reliable spell checkers. Unfortunately, they are often not used to the extent that they should be used.

Abbreviations and acronyms should be avoided unless the procedures analyst is certain the reader will understand their usage. When in doubt, spell it out. If abbreviations are used, they should be spelled out the first time they are used, with the abbreviation placed in parentheses immediately following the spelled-out words. For example, a policy section could begin with "It is the policy of Management Information Limited (MIL) to . . . " The abbreviation MIL could then be used consistently throughout the document instead of spelling it out each time. This rule also applies to acronyms.

Punctuation marks are signs used in the English writing system to separate groups of words and to convey some indication of the varying pitch and volume and especially the pauses in the flow of speech sounds. It is typically governed by its function, which is to make the procedures analyst's meaning clear, to promote ease of reading, and in varying degrees, to contribute to the total writing style.

Verb Tenses

The procedures analyst should be consistent by maintaining the same verb tense throughout the policy or procedure. The present tense is normally used; the simple present tense represents action occurring in the present without any indication of time deviation. On occasion, the more appropriate tense is the future or the past. Preferably, the policy or the procedure should be written in the third person. A shift in person should be avoided when writing policies or procedures. The *first person* is I or We; the *second person* is you; and the *third person* is he, she, one, anyone, person, or they. On a rare occasion, it may be acceptable to use the second person, *you*, in technical instructions. The first person should never be used.

Sentence Structure and Choice of Words

In the early draft stages, whole sentences can go awry. Fused sentences, comma faults, and sentence fragments are the sentence errors that most severely dislocate the continuity of the writing. Every sentence should proceed naturally from the one that it follows. There should be no contradictions. Sentences should be concisely worded and comprehensive in meaning. Sentences should be kept to 20 words or less.

The paragraph is the basic building block of any writing effort. Careful structuring of paragraphs reflects the writer's accurate thinking and logical organization. Each paragraph develops a logical unit of thought and is logically related to the paragraph that precedes it and to the paragraph that follows. Paragraph length should be tailored to the reader's convenience. The first sentence in any paragraph should express the main idea. The concluding sentence should be carefully worded and brief.

Gender Words

Until recently, writers have been trying to avoid the use of *he* because it implies a masculine bias. The current trend is to use the traditional *he* instead of the wordy, *he or she* phrase that gets old very quickly and is awkward to say in conversation. *He* is used throughout this book for convenience only. Wherever possible, the use of *he* should be avoided and generic terms should be used. For example, while I have used *he* throughout, I have also used terms such as *procedures analyst, forms analyst, cross-functional team, team leader, team player, user,* or *employee* to avoid this gender problem.

In countries where there are no equal opportunity laws, the procedures analyst should use either feminine or masculine words, depending on which group (male or female) is dominant. The procedures analyst should consider the nature of the laws and the customs of the country when selecting word groupings for policies and procedures.

Editing

A general review of your draft policy and procedure is recommended. As much as many of us despise rereading what we have written, I highly recommend it. Many types of errors can be caught during this kind of rereading exercise. Instead of concentrating on the whole document at once, consider reviewing the content of each section. If other procedures analysts are available, ask for a peer review of your draft documents. I used to think that I could write a perfect document every time. I used to write a draft and submit it for approval without any editing. It was only after I started to proofread my work that I realized that I was not perfect and I made lots of mistakes. In fact, my writing style improved immensely after I began to proofread my documents. I began to catch common mistakes. It is not all right to submit a "flawed" document to users or to management for review. As a procedures analyst, you should be submitting the highest quality possible. After all, it is your reputation and credibility that will suffer if you submit inferior documents for review and approval. Refer to my book, "7 Steps to Better Written Policies and Procedures" for three editing checklists that address questions about grammar, sentence structure, and other hard-to-notice errors. This book will also prove beneficial as it provides step-by-step guidelines for writing each section of the 7-section writing format.

Summary

Policies and procedures should be written using the best rules of English available. They should be simple, plain, impersonal and factual, characterized by a calm and restrained tone. There should be no attempt to arouse the reader's emotions. Good judgment in choosing the variety of English is one of the signs of a practiced and mature procedures analyst. If a message lacks clarity, it is useless because it cannot be properly interpreted. It is much more important that the procedures analyst attempt to express ideas clearly and simply, rather than attempting to impress the reader with length and complexity.

Chapter 6

DRAFT COORDINATION AND APPROVALS

Rough Draft Phase

Before a rough draft can be written, the appropriate writing format and the preferred numbering system should be selected. The format and the examples presented in Chapter 4 should be kept in mind when writing the initial draft. The writing format has been specifically designed for the procedures analyst to gather information from the research phase and insert it into each of the seven sections. Coupled with the writing style in Chapter 5, the procedures analyst should be able to draft meaningful sentence and word flow from the information inserted into each section.

When the procedures analyst commences the first rough draft, he needs to be careful as to how the guidelines are presented. If the guidelines are too broad, they may fail to coordinate people whose work interlocks, or overlaps. This approach could result in chaos for the users. If the guidelines, on the other hand, are too narrow, they may limit decisions. If the guidelines are too rigid, they can be hard to change once established. The procedures analyst should be careful to select an approach that is neither too rigid nor too broad. Writing policies and procedures becomes an art, a skill that can be learned.

After the first draft of the policy or procedure is written, it should be set aside for a couple of days. The draft document could then be reread and the appropriate changes made, if any. It is rare for any writer to be perfect the first time. The document should be checked for punctuation, unity, coherence, and transition. The procedures analyst should reconvene with his cross-functional team to review this draft and discuss changes. While this step will take additional time, it will prove most beneficial when trying to gain policy or procedure acceptance within the company. When the procedures analyst becomes accustomed to the recommended writing format, he may find that the first draft can be easily corrected, thus eliminating the need to rewrite the entire draft document.

With a fairly good draft, the procedures analyst should then give the draft document a title, assign a policy or procedure number and/or a revision number, and decide the appropriate review process. The review process will typically include user review, management review, and final approval sign-off. Infrequently, the user review could be ignored if the policy or procedure topic has been written exclusively by management. Examples of these types of documents include sensitive subjects like *Vision and Mission Statements*, *Sexual Harassment*, or *Nepotism*. In these cases, the final review and approval could reside entirely with the CEO/President and his staff.

Review Process

The review process for the majority of policies and procedures will include reviews by the users of the process, senior management, and the Policies and Procedures Department. The final approval of a policy or procedure document will typically be the CEO/President of the company. These reviews should be done formally using some kind of review form for record keeping purposes. The procedures analyst can design a form for routing the policy or procedure document or the procedures analyst can set up a standard email letter to those on these review lists. In either case, the procedures analyst should strive to use the same type of review form for both user review and management review.

Coordination Form or Memorandum

The procedures analyst should design a form or memorandum (or email) to be used to collect responses during the user and management reviews. Throughout most of my career, I have always used a form that could be routed through the mail, and more recently, one that could be routed through email. In any event, a standard form or memorandum should be created to ensure consistency of response and action. For a printed document, the draft document can be attached to this form or memorandum. In the case of an email, the file containing the draft document could be attached to the email questions. The information required on this special form or memorandum include, but are not limited to:

1	Name and location of the appropriate user or manager.
2	Brief summary of draft document subject matter.
3	Time limit for returning the draft document, normally within seven calendar days.
4	Request for one of four questions be answered: A. I CONCUR with no changes. B. I CONCUR IN GENERAL, with few non-critical changes. C. I DO NOT CONCUR. D. I DEFER COMMENTS.
5	Signature of reader responding to the review (user or management)

User Review Group

The *User Review Group* should include any individual identified as a user of a policy or procedure. Typically, the user group is selected from those individuals with positions below the position of senior management. One noteworthy option is to use a Policy and Procedure Review Committee for this purpose. One pitfall of user review is that the procedures analyst tends to overlook some users because he is unfamiliar with their involvement with the draft document. Much of this neglect can be avoided by discussing the results of the user reviews with the cross-functional team that was originally involved with the draft policy or procedure document during the research phase.

Once the draft document has been forwarded to the appropriate users, the procedures analyst will wait until the due date before taking additional action. If all the comments are not received on the scheduled return date, he should contact the users who are delinquent with their review copies. Though tempting, the procedures analyst should be careful about making threats about noncompliance because it can create poor rapport and morale. For example, the statement, "If the draft document is not returned within three days following the deadline, then the changes will be implemented," is often regarded by users as being unfair on the part of the procedures analyst. Enemies are not necessary in this job. The procedures analyst should always try to gain friends, not lose them.

While the draft document is being routed to the users, the document should be presented to the procedures analyst's supervisor for review. It is always possible that something has been overlooked and the supervisor can probably point out those areas that may require additional research before the document is routed to management for final review.

Responding to User Review Comments

When the draft documents have been returned, the comments should be reviewed to decide if additional research should be conducted before the draft document is forwarded to the Management Review group. If a review comment would result in a major change. The procedures analyst should arrange to meet with that user to discuss the changes. If conflicts continue to arise, then a meeting should be held to openly discuss the problems and to develop a joint solution. If conflict still exists, then the procedures analyst should review the situation with his supervisors. Preferably, an agreement or compromise can be reached at this level. Otherwise, the procedures analyst could make a note of this conflict and discuss it with the final approval authority during the final review.

All user review comments should be filed either in a physical file or electronically for at least one year. This file is useful backup in case of repercussions regarding the draft documents at a later date.

Management Review Group

Once there has been consensus among the users with the proposed draft document and any necessary changes have been incorporated, the procedures analyst should route the document to senior management. It is good business practice to route the draft to ALL members of management who are considered part of senior management regardless if the proposed draft affects them or not. This practice of routing all draft documents may seem strange, but surprisingly enough, some of those managers may have extensive experience. You just never know which manager will have valuable insights to a business process.

Routing proposed policies and procedures to senior management is a formal process and personal visits should not be made unless there is nonconcurrence after the comments are returned to the procedures analyst. If the document were routed to each manager in sequence, the review of a single document could take months depending on the number of members within senior management. Management should place some trust in the procedures analyst and rely on his judgment concerning the comments that are being returned.

If the review copies of the draft document are not returned on the indicated date, the procedures analyst should contact all those individuals who are late and discuss the deadline. It is not a serious problem if a user fails to meet a deadline and his comments are ignored. However, when management is involved, it may not be politically correct to ignore them. This is a difficult part of the process. How you plan to handle late responses from management should be decided upon with your own management in advance.

When the memorandum is sent to senior management, the distribution should also include the CEO/President. This practice of sending documents simultaneously to the CEO/President is very important because it is a time saver for the review process. If the CEO/President is not in agreement with a draft policy or procedure document, he can often discuss the issue in one of his staff meetings. If the procedures analyst routes this draft to the CEO/President AFTER the document has been reviewed by his management, their review time may have been wasted if the CEO/President finds a problem with the document. In this case, either the CEO/President will make a decision on the policy or procedure document or he will ask that it be rerouted for a second review based on his observations.

Attorney Review

If your company has an in-house corporate attorney, this individual should also be included in the management review process. If access to counsel is not available, then those policies and procedures that are particularly susceptible to legal questions or to government regulations (e.g., employee benefits, personnel issues, or security issues) should be submitted to outside counsel for review and advice.

Responding to Management Review Comments

If you have followed my suggestions regarding the types of questions asked of management regarding the draft document, then they will have reviewed the document and will have checked one of four choices. Briefly, these choices have the following meaning:

1. If they check, I CONCUR, it means that the draft document is satisfactory and the reader has nothing further to add.
2. If they check, I CONCUR IN GENERAL, it means that they generally agree with the contents but they have a few non-critical changes. The procedures analyst should evaluate the response and decide if the changes are necessary.
3. If they check, I DO NOT CONCUR, SEE SUMMARY, it means that they do not concur. In this case, the procedures analyst should discuss the problem with the individual who disagrees. It is important that a mutual agreement be reached regarding the nonconcurrence.
4. If they check, I DEFER COMMENT, it means that they have no opinion and will accept the comments of the other reviewers.

Once all comments have been received and resolved, changes can be incorporated into the draft document. The procedures analyst will then be able to submit the final draft document to the individual who has been delegated final approval authority. I have had several personal examples where management has accused me of incorporating changes that were not referenced on their review copy. These file copies were used to show management that I had presented them the correct information and that I had incorporated their comments.

All comments should be retained for at least one year. While it is rare to be challenged after a policy or procedure has been carried out, it can happen and it can be embarrassing if you cannot prove why a particular change was made, or not made. Take my advice, keep the comments for at least one year.

Final Approval Authority

This term may be new to some of you. *Final approval authority* refers to the individual who has final sign-off authority of all policies and procedures. In my 28 years of experience working in several multinational companies, I have found that it is best if the final approval authority is the CEO/President of the company. Throughout the years, I have tried varying management levels for approval, but when it comes to employees believing in the policy or procedure, it is more effective when the CEO/President has signed the document. You may ask if it is a good idea to have the vice president of a department sign off on a policy or procedure that has been written specifically for their area? While this idea seems to have merit, I have found that the CEO/President is the best person to make final approvals, if possible. It is sometimes physically impossible. Other times, the CEO/President has placed trust in his subordinates by delegating this responsibility. In either case, he should communicate his decision and support for the policies and procedures function to employees. Credibility is critical to the implementation of policies and procedures.

The person to whom final authority approval has been designated will also be in a position to offer advice to the procedures analyst. He will help those with any disputes on the subject. This person becomes the sounding board for the procedures analyst.

Approval Signatures on Policies or Procedures

While I have experimented with different approval signatures on policies and procedures, I think that an excellent final approval grouping is the (1) originator of the policy or procedure, (2) procedures analyst, and (3) final approval authority. If the originator is the procedures analyst, this approval would not be required.

Procedures Review Cycle

For the procedures analyst to be effective, it is imperative that he also approve the final draft document of the policy or procedure. The reasons are simple:

1. CREDIBILITY: If the CEO/President has made it known that he will not sign a policy or procedure unless the document has been thoroughly coordinated and reviewed by the procedures analyst first, then this will convey to the employees that the CEO/President has complete faith in the procedures analyst.

2. RECOGNITION: Once the credibility of the procedures analyst becomes known, the presence of this signature will be very important because it means that the policy or procedure has undergone a rigorous review and should represent the best solution at the time.

3. REFERENCE: Once the procedures analyst is recognized and known to be a representative of the CEO/President, employees will start asking the procedures analyst for interpretations of the policies and procedures.

Final Review and Document Sign-off

Once the document has been signed by the originator and the procedures analyst, the draft document can then be presented to the final approval authority for final review and approval. Upon approval, the procedures analyst will start making preparations for distribution, implementation, and training.

Summary

The procedures analyst has now written a reasonably sound draft of a policy or procedure document. The draft has been generally accepted and all of the major conflicts have been resolved. All of the changes have been incorporated into the final policy or procedure document. The document has been approved by the originating department, procedures analyst, and the CEO/President. The policy or procedure is now ready for distribution and implementation.

Chapter 7

DISTRIBUTION METHODS

Distribution of Printed and On-line Documents

There are several ways to distribute policies and procedures for printed documents, the most standard method being the printed company manual. With on-line documents, distribution can be routinely set up through an email system or web page. The on-line manual is the focus of Chapter 10. The purpose of this chapter will be a discussion of the printed company manual. The majority of businesses today still use printed policies and procedures.

Many companies with on-line and web capabilities use a dual-manual system of both printed and electronic manuals. In fact, I currently work at a large telecommunications company and we have printed manuals, on-line manuals, an Intranet, an Extranet, and even printed and electronic forms. The decision as to whether you want to use printed or electronic documentation, or both, will probably be decided by users and management.

Printed Company Manual

A manual can be defined as *a book(s) containing approved policies and procedures* that represents records of decisions or standards. This collection of documents will be referred to as a *company manual*. A company manual is intended to be used by the employees of an organization. If the manual is not made accessible to all users, much of the value could be lost. A manual could be one binder, or many, depending on the content covered and on the total system established by the Policies and Procedures Department. There are several important decisions that need to be made when creating a manual system including the type of binder to be used, index dividers, and the sequence of content within the manual.

Binder Selection

Policy and procedure documents may be assembled into a variety of binder types, the most common being the loose-leaf binder (also called a standard ring binder). Others, like the comb, prong, or post binders, are available but not practical for a policies and procedures manual. The company manual needs to be easily picked up, opened, and scanned for information. It needs to stand up easily on a shelf or table. It should be easy to insert and replace documents when necessary.

The loose-leaf binder meets these characteristics and is the type that I recommend. There are several types of ring mechanisms; the slant ring is the most efficient ring mechanism. It holds 25% more documents than standard ring binders. This slant ring has been angled for optimum sheet movement. With this special shape, pages do not jam or curl. Bunching of sheets can be prevented when the covers are closed and the binder lies flat. It is especially convenient because the binder can be closed with ease, no matter how many documents are in the manual. The only drawback to the slant binder is its cost. It is more expensive than the standard round ring binder.

The type of looseleaf binder selected (slant or round ring) depends on the number of potential manual holders, the volume of estimated policies and procedures, and the budget allocated to support the policies and procedures functions. The capacity, ring mechanism, cover construction, and labeling should be considered in the analysis.

Capacity of Binder

The capacity of the binder is dependent on the estimated number of policies and procedures to be placed into a manual. For the standard binder, the ring capacity is one to three inches. As a rule of thumb, there are 50 sheets of paper plus the index divider for each 1/4" of ring size. For example, if there are 50 procedures, each four pages in length, then the binder selected should have at least the capacity to hold 200 pages. This would be equal to a ring size of one inch. The ring size is the determining factor for the ring capacity. It is a common mistake to measure the spine width when deciding the binder size. The capacity can be calculated by measuring the largest inner diameter of a ring. It is recommended that future additions be estimated. This is often where procedures analysts make a mistake. They tend to look at the cost versus the true capacity needed. Thus, they will buy one-inch manuals where the long-term thinker would buy three-inch manuals for the current requirement of one inch capacity. This may not seem important at first but as the binder reaches its capacity, the procedures analyst will wish he had heeded my warnings.

Construction of Binder

The construction of a binder is a major cost consideration. Binders are normally constructed of smooth or grained vinyl, imitation leather, pressboard, chipboard, genuine leather, canvas, or molded plastic. The most common surface is vinyl. Vinyl binders can be padded on the front, back, and spine and they can be imprinted with the company's name in color. Manuals for policies and procedures should be constructed of stiff material. These binders can be placed upright on desks, shelves, or on filing cabinets. If a flexible material is used, the manual should lie flat because it will be flimsy and will not stand up well. These flimsy binders are often shuffled under papers or in drawers and out of sight. This is why it is important that these manuals can stand up on their own on a desk or bookshelf. A manual has a better chance of being used if it is visible!

Vinyl binders with clear plastic overlays are the preferred binder for creating an attractive manual. This allows for insertion of materials for a professional, customized look. It is easy to create attractive binders by using colored paper with black text or by using white paper with colored ink and graphics. I prefer a dark color with white text.

The front of the binder would contain the title of the policy or the procedure and possibly the company's logo. The spine would contain the title of the policy or procedure. The back could be a non-printed sheet of colored paper inserted to make the manual appear to be one color when viewed from a distance while sitting on a shelf or bookcase. These colored covers can be quickly produced on a photocopier instead of being professionally printed, thus cutting the cost even more. When the title of the manual changes, then only the front and spine cover would need to be changed.

One major advantage of using a binder with clear plastic overlays is that manuals can be color coded. This makes it easy for users to identify specific manuals. For example, the Human Resources Manual could be green; the Accounting Manual could be red; and the Engineering Manual could be blue. With the current technology, it is quite possible to produce some interesting and very attractive artwork for these manuals using current personal computers.

Index Tab Dividers

The documents inside the manuals need to be organized with some type of dividers for quick and easy reference purposes. There are several types of dividers that may be considered. An index tab divider should extrude past the edge of the sheets you are separating so that the tabs can be easily seen and used. Index dividers contain precut plastic tabs that can be typed, handwritten, or laser printed. Each tab should be labeled with the corresponding section heading from the table of contents. Typically, these sections are numbers or text. If you have elected to select a series of numbers for each section, the main series number will be printed on the tab. For example, if you have identified the series 1000-1999 for Administration, then the number 1000 would be printed on the tab. While you can elect to type a name of a department on the tab, it can cause frequent changes as any change in a department name will necessitate a change in your tabs. Thus, I would highly recommend the use of numbers instead of departments. There are many types of tab dividers available. I suggest visiting a local stationary store or discussing this issue with your binder supplier.

Sheet Lifters

No manual is complete without sheet lifters and yet few people have ever heard of or have seen sheet lifters. Sheet lifters are those plastic strips you sometimes see in the front and back of manuals. They are very useful. They actually help a manual full of documents close easily. They are hole punched and are available as both curved and flat. I prefer the flat sheet lifters. They are more efficient. Sheet lifters are placed on the top and bottom of the documents inside the manual.

Copying the Approved
Policy or Procedure

Once the company manual binder type has been selected, obtained, and distributed to designated manual holders, there are certain steps that should be taken to prepare approved policies and procedures for distribution. First, the *date* on which the policy or procedure is to be effective should be selected. Typically, the date is the same date on which the policies and procedures are photocopied and distributed. The policies or procedures should never be distributed before the effective date. The date should be printed on all pages of the policy or procedure including those pages that contain exhibits, illustrations, or forms. Second, the *Revision History* section of the writing format should be updated. Third, the numerical, alphabetical, and keyword tables of contents should be updated to reflect the new, or revised policy or procedure.

When the documents are finally ready to be photocopied and distributed to the manual holders, the procedures analyst should put the original documents into some kind of order. I prefer the following set of documents when copying policies or procedures for distribution.

1. Distribution Letter
2. Mailing List
3. Numerical, Alphabetical, and Keyword Table of Contents
4. Policy or Procedure Document

When the policies and procedures are finally distributed to the manual holders, the procedures analyst should ensure that the current policy or procedure is discarded and the new, or revised draft document is inserted in the proper section. Some type of standard "Distribution Announcement Letter" should be designed that clearly explains what should be done with revised documents. It is the responsibility of the manual holder to ensure that his people receive a copy and/or ensure that they understand its contents. Employees are expected to fulfill their responsibilities according to the requirements as stated in the policy or procedure. This is a key point and is often overlooked or abused by those that receive policies and procedures. The recipient of approved policies or procedures will often decide which documents will be shown to his subordinates. I do not agree with this philosophy. I think that the employee should be shown all approved policies and procedures and it should be his choice whether to read or ignore them. This is one of the main reasons that the procedures analyst should find alternate methods of communication and to incorporate training classes when possible.

Distribution Announcement Letter

When distributing policies and procedures, a *distribution announcement letter* (form, memorandum, or email) should be prepared. This letter would contain a summary of the policies or procedures being distributed and instructions on how to remove the previous revision and where to insert the new table of contents and the approved policy or procedure. A form, memorandum, or email message, would be an acceptable medium.

For those companies with email systems, notice of new policies and procedures can be emailed to all employees. The policy or procedure (in read-only mode) for on-line manuals or the Intranet could be attached to this email message; or a location on the network could be referenced.

Mailing List

The distribution of company manuals and those policies and procedures contained therein should be coordinated by the policies and procedures analyst. Selecting those persons who will be on mailing lists to receive company policies and procedures is more difficult than it seems. On the surface, it would appear that anything less than a total employee distribution would be inequitable because employees are expected to follow current policies and procedures when performing their assigned job responsibilities. However, a total distribution of policies and procedures is impractical, expensive, and very difficult to achieve in a timely manner.

Recent litigation cases sometimes make it difficult to distribute policies and procedures to a companywide distribution list. When these documents are distributed, it is very difficult to ensure that the manual holder receives, reads, understands, and files the policy or procedure in the correct spot within a manual. If the contents of the policy or procedure change and the employees are not properly informed, they may be inclined to follow those policies or procedures that are currently in their manuals. Litigation cases have shown that even if the policies and procedures are published but somehow never get into the hands of the employee, the court will tend to favor the employee's side by referring to the employee's outdated copy versus the most current one. In other words, if there were a companywide distribution system, then it becomes the company's responsibility to be absolutely certain that each employee reads, understands, and files the latest issue of every policy or procedure published. This goal is very difficult to achieve even in a small company with few policies and procedures.

From a company standpoint, it seems that policy and procedure manuals should be restricted to those individuals who manage a function. This is generally equated to all management and some professional individuals. From an employee standpoint, all employees should be informed about changes to company policies or procedures. The procedures analyst should work with management to decide an equitable solution to ensure that the cost of producing manuals for distribution is not prohibitive as well as to ensure that all employees have access to company policies and procedures.

Once the company manual distribution list has been decided, the procedures analyst can use a distribution log which may be used for two purposes: (1) as a mailing list and (2) as a check off list when a policy or a procedure is distributed to a manual holder.

Table of Contents

The table of contents, or front matter, can be divided into numerical, alphabetical, and keywords. Each should be updated every time a change is made to the manual. While all three are not required in your manual, they make it easier for the reader to find information. With on-line manuals, this table of contents is no longer an issue because of random search capabilities. It becomes a matter of typing in a keyword, with the result being a list of policies and procedures that contain this keyword. This kind of search is not feasible in a printed company manual.

A numerical table of contents is sorted in ascending numerical order. An alphabetical table of contents is sorted alphabetically. The keyword table of contents lists all major points of each policy or procedure arranged in alphabetical order. Examples of a numerical and alphabetical table of contents are shown in Appendices F and G.

Central Repository
for Policies and Procedures

Employees should have complete access to a set of policies and procedures. Many companies will set up a system of policies and procedures and make regular distribution to a predetermined list of individuals. However, if these manual holders do not make their manuals accessible to any employee in their area, then these employees will not have an opportunity to read new, or revised, policies and procedures. Therefore, the manual loses much of its value.

There is a solution to this problem. Namely, a central repository could be set up for all policies and procedures. A central location could be selected to maintain a complete set of company manuals. This set of manuals should have its own manual holder so that its contents can be kept up to date. Locations could include the company copying center, the company library, the cafeteria, the lobby, or a popular location where many employees frequently visit or pass by.

Alternate Methods of Distribution

Besides the company manual, the procedures analyst should use as many communication techniques as possible to distribute the contents of policies and procedures. Many employees are typically left out of distribution lists. Manual holders often fail to disseminate policies and procedures distributed to them. Possible alternatives include, but are not limited to: company bulletins, company newsletters, company memoranda, email messages, or training classes. These are just a few of the more common ones.

Company Bulletins

The company bulletin can be defined as an *official employee communication medium used to communicate items of general interest.* Bulletins are normally associated with bulletin boards, but they can also be mailed to employees, as well as being posted on bulletin boards throughout the company. Examples of bulletins include important procedural changes, holiday schedule, new benefits, new form being issued, and other general information that can be posted on a single page. The format of these bulletins is your choice. Preferably you should try to use large letters and graphics as attention-getters to those passing by. While bulletins are typically one-page, they could be longer. These bulletins could be called a different name in your organization, but the purpose of the information posted is the same.

Policies and procedures are not the only items referenced on a bulletin board, so the boards should be controlled by a department such as Human Resources or Administration. A system should be established in which anything hung on a bulletin board has to be approved by the predetermined department. Otherwise, employees are apt to post anything they want and thus, degrade the board. I have seen complete copies of policies and procedures hung on bulletin boards as well. While this is a good means of communication, it is difficult to maintain the currency of these copies. If this method is used, you might consider using colored paper as an attention-getter.

Company Newsletters

The company newspaper is a publication provided by the employer. Its primary purpose is to keep employees informed about the company, its operations, and its policies. Not all organizations have a regular company newspaper. For those organizations that do publish a newspaper fairly regularly, the procedures analyst should arrange with the editor of the newspaper to print the titles of the policies and procedures as they are approved or revised. Those policies and procedures that may be of interest to most of the employees could be highlighted with a short summary. The procedures analyst could also volunteer to become a reporter for the company newsletter.

Company Memoranda

If a company does not have a newspaper and/or if a policy or a procedure contains subject matter that should reach all employees, then the procedures analyst could write a memorandum highlighting a policy or a procedure. Often this memorandum will have more impact than a bulletin because the memorandum is generally signed by the person with final approval authority for policies and procedures. The memorandum could be directed to the department administrative staff for distribution to those in the department. It could be attached to or inserted into pay envelopes, or it could be mailed to the employee's home address. The main advantage of this method of distribution is that it is fairly certain to reach most of the employees and their families. The main disadvantage is that once the memorandum is read, it is normally discarded. Most policies and procedures should be read at least twice to fully assimilate their content.

Email Messages

Email is a form of electronic communication. It is offered in almost all computer network systems. It is a very efficient method of sending and receiving mail among employees. When I first started using email almost ten years ago, the number of printed memoranda that I produced or received were reduced significantly. In fact, many employees were known to put aside printed documents and read them when they got a chance. Email was more important to them.

With email, the distribution of important policies and procedures and highlights has become very easy and efficient because documents can be attached to an email message. It is also possible to create a "returned receipt" for an email. Thus, you can be assured that at least the recipient has received the mail. You can never be certain that the email, or attachment, is read and understood.

Some readers might ask why all policies and procedures are not simply distributed through email. As has already been explained, a set of policies and procedures needs to be available to any employee. Some companies will have both a printed set of manuals and an electronic set either on the network or on the web. A complete set of current documents should be retained in a central repository for historical and legal reasons.

This set of documents should be retained in both printed and electronic file formats. Each time the policy and procedure documents are updated, the historical file should also be updated with a new version. The documents should not be overwritten. Historical versions should be retained.

Training

While training is not viewed as a distribution document like email or a newsletter, it should fall into the same category. Training is a very important communication tool for policies and procedures. Distributing a company manual is usually not enough. Communicating the content through various alternate methods is usually not enough; but with training, there is a likelihood that the employees can be reached. Training provides an interactive teaching tool. This is perhaps the best and most thorough way that the user can assimilate the content of a new, or revised, policy or procedure. Training is the primary focus of Chapter 8.

Summary

The establishment of different methods of distribution is the main focus of this chapter. The advantages and disadvantages of the printed company manual are emphasized because the printed manual is still used in many companies today. While on-line manuals are being adopted by many companies, it will be decades before small companies eliminate the printed manual. Companies will generally have some kind of dual-manual system, with some policies and procedures in an electronic format and some in printed manuals.

The newspaper, bulletin, memorandum, email, and training are alternate methods of distributing policies and procedures to employees. These methods should only be used to reinforce ideas already presented in the policy or procedure. Different communication methods should be tried and the results analyzed to find the best combination of communication media in order to reach the majority of persons affected.

Chapter 8

IMPLEMENTATION AND TRAINING

Implementation Guidelines

A policy or procedure is considered implemented when it is distributed to the manual holders. Although this does not take into consideration whether or not the policy or procedure has been read and understood. When you think of the word *implement* you think of phrases like, "to carry out," "bring about," or "execute." The word *implementation* means "accomplishment" or "achievement." It may be an achievement to distribute a policy or procedure, but the real accomplishment comes when the user understands the content and follows its guidelines. How understanding comes about is the focus of this chapter.

There are two very effective means to ensure a policy or procedure is understood. The first is the use of *control points* and the second is through *training*. A **control point** is a person or department that can have the effect of ensuring that a policy or procedure is followed by becoming the "watchdog" of the guidelines. For example, if the procedure directs a person to complete an expense report in a certain way and to route it to the appropriate department for approval, the department receiving that expense report becomes the control point. They can insist that the expense report be properly completed according to the policy or procedure. Of it does not comply, the "watchdog" will reject and return the expense report to the requester. In other words, this person (or department) will explain the correct rules and regulations to those who are in violation, or refer them to the correct policy or procedure. One suggestion for the "watchdog" is to assign this task to one, or several members of the original cross-functional team.

The second implementation method is through **training**. Studies have shown that if people are properly trained shortly after the distribution of policies or procedures they will become more effective. It is the repetition and reinforcement of ideas presented during training that will enable the employee to assimilate the information more quickly than learning by trial and error. It is highly recommended that the procedures analyst develop some kind of training program for the implementation of approved policies and procedures while the approved document is being planned for distribution. The procedures analyst should also consider some form of mentoring and coaching for helping those trained to assimilate the training material into their daily work routine. Refer to my book, "Achieving 100% Compliance of Policies and Procedures" for entire chapters on training, mentoring, coaching, and communication programs.

Benefits of Training

The purpose of any training program is to deliver results. The goal is for people to be more effective after training than before. Training in an organization can be defined as *the formal process used to develop in an employee the attitudes, knowledge, and skills that make him capable of effective performance.* Training focuses specifically on the employee's performance on a given job. The employee should be motivated to want to use his ability in accomplishing organizational goals. A trained employee needs less time to carry out assignments. He should be able to achieve job proficiency sooner than if he had not been properly trained. Many day-to-day demands on management would be lessened if the subordinates were more self-sufficient. Some benefits of training are listed below:

1. Greater gratification from job;
2. Increased job security and earnings;
3. More opportunity for advancement;
4. Self-respect and the respect of others; and
5. Sense of mastery or proficiency.

A reasonable hypothesis is that those who increase in knowledge and grow in behavior will in the final analysis make better employees with stronger feelings of satisfaction about their work and about their relationships on the job. The ultimate goal of education and training is mastery, or job proficiency.

Management cannot escape the responsibility for training. It is essential to success. The responsibility for carrying out all policies and procedures is shared by management. It is to their benefit that employees understand the intent of policies and procedures. As management understands more about policies and procedures and more information is communicated to employees, less time needs to be spent handling day-to-day problems. Despite how persistently senior management advocates or directs that policies and procedures are communicated to employees, management never seems to have enough time to sit down and discuss such matters with subordinates. Helping others may be a time-consuming task, but steps should be taken so that the majority of employees comprehend the guidelines established in a policy or procedure.

The procedures analyst has the important responsibility of helping management in training employees. Generally, the Policies and Procedures Department will be responsible for training that is related to policies and procedures. In large companies that have training departments, the instructor could be a professional trainer.

The Learning Process

When a person is in the process of being trained, that person is undergoing a learning process. Learning can be defined as *the changes of behavior resulting from practice*. Learning can occur with a single contact, but normally it is done through repetition and reinforcement. How a person learns and/or perceives information should be considered when preparing speeches for training classes. Some general guidelines include:

1. People learn at different rates;
2. A person's attention span is between 20 and 30 minutes;
3. People retain more through repetition and feedback;
4. Difficult-to-learn tasks require the close attention of the instructor;
5. People tend to remember more at the beginning or ending of a speech;
6. Learning takes place quicker if the person is willing to learn;
7. Replacing a bad habit with a good habit requires more time and effort than learning a good habit;

8. A person who receives a message can only interpret it in terms of his own experiences; and
9. Learning is eased if material is organized into a logical plan.

Preparation for Training Classes

Once an approved policy or procedure has been distributed, the procedures analyst can begin the preparatory process for training classes. The size of the class, the number of classes, and the thoroughness of the presentation will depend chiefly on the budget allocated to training classes. When setting up training classes, there are many action items to be performed. The procedures analyst must:

1. Select the subject matter and decide the purpose of the training class;
2. Decide the location where the class will be held;
3. Decide the number of persons who will be attending training classes;
4. Decide the time length of a class;
5. Publish a training schedule;
6. Analyze the audience;
7. Gather material and illustrations;
8. Make outline;
9. Select and prepare visual aids;
10. Select type of speaking method;
11. Choose method of speaking;
12. Prepare the presentation;
13. Practice speech aloud;
14. Deliver the presentation; and
15. Ask for feedback to presentation.

Subject Matter and Purpose

The subject matter of the training class will normally be an approved policy or procedure. Depending on the interests of the audience, it may be possible that only the highlights should be presented. The procedures analyst will use his discretion about which policies and procedures are presented. Often the extent of the content to be presented, the potential number of participants, and the estimated overall length of the training class are factors in deciding which policies and procedures become topics of training classes. Any time an implemented policy or procedure becomes a problem to those using it, the appropriate policies and procedures should be examined to decide if a training class is needed.

Classroom Location(s)

It is preferable if possible, to have all the training classes for a specific topic in the same location. If this is not feasible, the procedures analyst may have to prepare several different presentations depending on the classroom available. If a video conferencing room is available, then the training class can be given in multiple locations at the same time.

The procedures analyst should try to ensure that the room selected is conducive to learning. The room should be large enough to accommodate 20 people comfortably. There should be adequate seating. How seating is arranged will depend on the type of speech to be used. If it is to be informal, then the chairs could be arranged in clusters around tables or arranged in a circle without tables. If it is to be formal, then the chairs could be arranged in rows.

The temperature of the room should be controllable. If the room becomes too hot, people become sleepy. If the room becomes too cold, people feel discomfort.

Number of Persons per Training Class

Once the location(s) has been selected, the total number of employees to be trained should be decided. This will have a bearing on the number of persons per training class. If there is a large number of employees and very little time to present the material, then the classes should be large. The number of employees per class will directly influence the type of speech selected. With a smaller number of employees per class, the class can be more personal and informal. Keep the classes to no more than 16 people.

Length of Class

The ideal length for a training class for policies and procedures is one hour with a five-minute rest period occurring halfway through the class.

Studies have shown that a person's attention span is between 20 and 30 minutes. If the subject matter being presented requires more than one hour, then additional follow-up classes should be scheduled. There is always the temptation to continue talking beyond the hour time limit, but the speaker should resist this temptation despite how attentive the audience may seem. Some people become clock-watchers when the end of a training class approaches and can become quite restless if the scheduled class time is exceeded. In all fairness to the other participants, the class should be halted. The careful speaker will watch the time so that he can adjust the speech to where there will be adequate time to give a summary. I might add that where I work now we have frequent videoconferencing meetings and when an hour is up, the video machines shut off, thus ending the meeting abruptly. While I am not in favor of this abrupt shutoff, it can be very effective for reminding the speakers to watch their time.

However, if the hour is reached and there is not much material left in the presentation, the speaker could announce that he plans to continue past the hour for a short time to conclude the material. There is no need for a second class when there is little remaining material to discuss. It would be a waste of time for the speaker and the audience to reconvene for five or ten minutes.

Training Schedule

The best times for training classes are the first and last hour of the day and during the lunch hour. The choice of overlapping work and non-work hours will be dependent on management's view of the benefit of these classes. If it is a benefit to the employee, the classes should be held after working hours or during the lunch period. If it is a benefit to the employer, the classes could be held during working hours. However, studies have shown that class size will greatly diminish if scheduled before or after working hours.

Supervisors should allow their employees to attend training classes if possible. Ideally, the procedures analyst should work out times with the affected supervisors so that the workload of their employees is the least affected. If this is not feasible, then either an early morning or late afternoon time is desirable. Early Monday morning or late Friday afternoon times are not desirable due to weekend blues or to weekend anticipation. Whatever time(s) is selected, the time(s) should not vary from day to day.

If the training classes are scheduled from week to week, then the same day should be kept whenever possible. Once the times and days are selected, a memorandum should be addressed to all participants indicating the subject matter to be discussed, purpose of the training class, classroom location(s), speaker, and time and day on which each employee is expected to attend. There should always be a provision for people who request alternate days and times.

Analysis of Audience

The audience will normally consist of all employees who come in contact with a policy or procedure in their daily activities. This could include anyone from the entry-level employee to the CEO/President. It could even include vendors, suppliers, or consultants. The total number of employees to be trained, size of the audience, average age, sex, occupations, educational background, social position, habits, likes and dislikes, or their membership affiliation are all factors that may influence how a presentation is prepared.

The procedures analyst should find out what the people want or value most, and what chiefly interests the audience. If the audience consists of management-level personnel, they can be presented the rationale for the procedure and how to administer it to their subordinates. The details of the procedure may be more appropriately presented to those office personnel who actually use the guidelines being established in the policy or procedure.

Gathering Material and Illustrations

Generally, additional material or illustrations are not needed because the subject matter is completely covered by the distributed policy or procedure. The primary handout is the policy or procedure document. Illustrations may be presented during the presentation as supportive material for the main points. Handouts and other supportive material should be handed out at the end of the training class. If the speaker has "slide notes," these could placed on the tables at the start of the class.

Though the policy or the procedure is prepared in an outline form, a new, briefer outline should be prepared. The approved policy or procedure reflects written English. The presentation should be in spoken English. Written English is formalized and impersonal. Spoken English allows for greater sentence and paragraph variety, more personal pronouns such as *I, we,* and *you*, slang, contractions, and repetition.

Ideas should be arranged in a clear and systematic order. The structure of the speech should be preserved by making sure that each point is directly related to a specific purpose. The outline compels the procedures analyst to critique his outline and to examine the supporting materials. It reveals flaws in reasoning and in the development of points. The outline will be used as the basis for the preparation of the speech once the basic type of speech is selected.

Visual Aids

Visual aids are teaching devices that require little or no reading to communicate meaning. They make possible a wide range of interesting, realistic, meaningful, and stimulating learning experiences. Learning becomes more meaningful because people can see what they are studying, rather than merely hearing. The procedures analyst should be careful not to let the visual aids dominate the topic.

People retain about 25 percent of what is heard, about 35 percent of what is seen, and about 50 percent of what is seen and heard. Communicating effectively in writing is often difficult, but communicating with the spoken word is even more difficult. Visual aids are often used to support a presentation. Spoken words can be dry and boring and you can lose the interest of the audience. When you movement, audio, or video aids are added to help support the speaker's ideas, the interest of the audience can be aroused.

PREPARATION OF VISUAL AIDS. Good visuals start with good originals. An original can be written, printed, or typed, but it should be large and very legible. Lettering has much to do with the effectiveness of the visual. Careless lettering can detract from even the best illustration, while neat, well-planned lettering can be effective by itself.

The size of lettering can be decided by the size of the room in which the presentation is being given. Lettering should be tall enough to be seen from the back of the room. The originals should be kept simple with a maximum of six or seven lines per page and with six or seven words per line. Tables are often used to present information because data can be arranged systematically in columns and rows. The procedures analyst should make sure that everyone can see and read the visual aids easily.

Two Categories of Visual Aids

Visual aids can be divided into nonprojected and projected media. Nonprojected media includes chalkboards, dry marker boards, and flip charts. Projected media include 35mm slides, overhead projectors, videotapes, and computer graphics.

The procedures analyst should select the type of visual aid that's best suited to the method of presentation. The budget amount allocated to training classes, subject matter being presented, number of people per class, size of the room selected, availability of well-placed electrical outlets, lighting conditions, and time assigned for the training classes are some factors that should be considered when selecting appropriate visual aids for training classes.

Chalkboards. The chalkboard is not recommended for use in a training class. Chalk is hard to write with, is messy, and if the procedures analyst needs to elaborate a point, it is difficult to write fast and neatly using chalk.

Dry Marker Boards. White boards are very popular for writing several points as you talk. They can also be used for issues as they occur during the training class or a meeting. When planning to use a white board, make sure that there is a supply of liquid chalk markers on hand. When writing on the board, keep your lettering large.

The dry marker board replaces the chalkboard in many aspects. The board is typically white and has a high-gloss, stain-resistant porcelain surface. A felt-tip, liquid-chalk marker is used. The image goes on wet and dries instantly. The markers typically come in a variety of colors.

Flip charts. A flip chart is a large writing pad often mounted on an easel. It can be used effectively to create real time visuals. It is ideal for procedure training classes because information can be written in advance and the pages flipped back so they are not revealed until the speaker is ready to use them. As archaic as they sound, they are very useful because they can be prepared in advance. It is also a good idea to diversify the visual aids and not just use one technique. Flip charts are especially useful if traveling to several locations for training because they can be brought along to the various locations and used again.

35mm Slides. While still pictures, or slides, are very effective for training and other types of presentations, I do not recommend them for procedural training. The use of slides is not recommended in a training class. Filming and developing can be expensive. If the photography is not up to professional grades, the quality of the slides can be distracting to the audience. The slide projector can be harmful to the presentation if improperly used. While I have seen slide projectors used in several churches for projecting constant information, I cannot recall them being used in any recent training classes.

Overhead projectors. The use of overhead projectors for training classes is highly recommended. It is probably the most widely used visual aids in the projector category. The room can be fairly well-lit while an overhead projector is being used. It is the standard method for projecting information many times larger onto a screen. The picture is transferred onto a clear film called a *transparency*. The transparency is placed on the projector and its image is transferred onto a screen or a wall.

The purpose of any overhead projector transparency is to visually support what the speaker is saying so that the message comes across quickly, clearly, and consistently. The size of the original image to be projected should be less than 8-1/2" x 11". The ideal image dimension to be projected is 7" x 9". The image can be projected either horizontally or vertically. Headlines, colors, or graphs can also be used. An overlay technique, color adhesive film, or shading can be used to enhance the original image.

A great feature of transparencies is that they can be produced directly from a personal computer. The resulting image is clear and crisp. This is a preferred method of transference. Another method is to photocopy the printed paper copy directly onto the transparency. The use of overhead projectors offers some advantages over other types of visual aids including:

1.   Presentations can be given to any size group and the room does not have to very dark;
2.   The procedures analyst can face the audience at all times;
3.   Each transparency can be revealed one-by-one and sections can be covered up; and
4.   Overhead transparencies can be made quickly and are relatively inexpensive.

Videotapes. Videotape can be used in much the same way as film but it offers one advantage: it can be shown in a fully lit room. Videotape can also be used in real time in the classroom. This can be especially useful if participants are doing a skill practice. Videotape also can be used to create in-house presentations that can be used in much the same way as films. The use of videos for training has advantages and disadvantages. Videos are especially useful when the procedures analyst has to reach a very large group of people and the topic can be filmed in advance. I remember with one procedure, "time-keeping," our customer required all employees to view the videotape at least once per year. In this case, a video is an excellent medium as it can be filmed in advance and no one needs to administer the video other than to start and stop the video cassette recorder. One of the chief problems with video is that the speaker cannot interact with the audience unless the video is used to supplement part of a training class.

Computer Graphics. Computer graphics are becoming increasingly popular. They can be developed and displayed on computer monitors. They can be used as an alternative to a slide presentation or even overhead transparencies. Programs can allow you to create visuals that can be displayed on a computer monitor in a sequence much like slides or film strips. They offer the additional advantage of providing some video-like effects, such as wipes, dissolves, and fades. Computer graphics can output from the computer into other types of presentation media. Basically, the procedures analyst creates a presentation software and hooks it to a special machine that projects the colorful, animated presentation onto a screen or monitor. The speaker can control the speed of the presentations using the keyboard or mouse.

As the subject of this book is not on training materials, I will leave the details of doing presentations using these various types of visual aids to the procedures analyst and those supporting him with the training class. There may be additional presentation techniques available for presenting policies and procedures to audiences. The availability of many different kinds of visual aids gives the procedures analyst the opportunity to create an interesting presentation using several methods. For example, a training class for expense reports could be presented with an overhead projector and a computer projection system.

Basic Types of Speeches

The ideal type of speech is one in which the listeners participate and from which they retain the most information. While this situation is ideal, there are often circumstances that dictate different types of presentations, or demand several kinds of presentation techniques within the same training course.

Lectures

Some form of lecturing is typically found in speeches. Lecturing is one-sided and the audience is passive. If the audience has little knowledge of a subject, then lecturing may be used throughout the class. If the audience is quite familiar with the subject, then lecturing may only be needed for part of the class. A question-and-answer period could be used for the rest of the class.

Question-and-Answers

The use of a question-and-answer period is a necessary part of training classes. The question period is the speaker's reward because it gives him feedback on the presentation. The speaker uses this feedback for self-evaluation for future training classes. Questions and answers help to fill in gaps, emphasize topics, and clarify misunderstandings. Questions can be presented very quickly to the audience or the speaker may give lengthy explanations or comments to inquisitive employees. Questions should be answered tactfully and with much detail.

Discussions

Often question-and-answer periods will lead to discussions. Discussions involve the exchange of ideas or information. The goal of a discussion is to reach an agreement or a decision. In this case, the speaker may pose a question and ask that the audience work out the answers among themselves. The speaker should get the discussion started, keep it from wandering, bring out essential facts, ensure that everyone participates, and summarize the important points as they occur. Discussions are beneficial because they are employee-oriented, issues are explored, and there is a free flow of arguments, questioning, and reasoning.

Methods of Speaking

There are five kinds of speeches that could be selected when delivering a speech about policies and procedures to an audience. The speaker should pick the speech type with which he is most comfortable. These include:

1. *Impromptu.* This type of speech is delivered at the spur of the moment. No specific preparation is made. The speaker relies totally on his knowledge and skill; he should organize ideas while speaking.
2. *Written.* This type of speech is read from notes that have been completely written out beforehand. The procedures analyst should try to think about what he is saying as it is being said. This kind of speech should only be used if the wording choice is critical.
3. *Memorized.* This type of speech is written out and committed to memory. When memorizing, one tends to concentrate on words rather than ideas. If interrupted, the entire speech may be forgotten. A lapse in memory can be embarrassing. Answering questions can be difficult if the speaker is not very familiar with the material. This type of speech should only be used if the procedures analyst is a nervous speaker.

4. *Improvised*. This type of speech is planned and outlined in detail; the draft is written out but the words are not memorized.
5. *Memorized-impromptu*. This type of speech is first written out and then memorized; however, it is presented as if it were impromptu.

This last type of speech is the one I prefer. It gives the impression that the speaker is aware of the material and is confident that it will go well. It is suited to nervous people and those who do not like to speak in front of crowds. The nervous person can write a speech down, memorize it, and then make it seem like it is a natural, unrehearsed presentation.

Speeches and training classes should be informative rather than persuasive. The procedures analyst aims to inform; he does not want to urge any particular belief or advise any particular action. His purpose is only to have the listeners understand and to provide them with the information needed for understanding. The procedures analyst will try to relate ideas or expand upon the existing knowledge of the audience. He should be sure that the structure of the speech is clear to encourage greater retention of information.

Wording the Speech

The speech should have three basic parts: introduction, main thesis, and summary. The *introduction* is used to get the attention of the audience, to motivate them to listen, to define the purpose, and to present a brief outline (agenda) of the subject matter. Catching the attention of the audience could be done with an unusual approach, a question, a story, a strong statement, an opinion, a statistic, or a quotation. The statement of purpose is critical to the speech and should not be taken lightly. During the introduction, the speaker should make an agreement with the audience as to when the question-and-answer period will be allowed.

The *main thesis* is the body of the speech. The purpose should be repeated. The main points should be presented and supported by illustrations, as applicable. An outline can be immensely useful in structuring the main thesis and in maintaining unity throughout the speech.

The *summary* is normally tied to the opening sentence. The key points should be restated. The speaker can go directly into either the question-and-answer period following the summary, or the question-and-answer period can precede the summary. Whichever occurs, the transition should be as smooth as possible.

The speech should have a clear organization of content. The most significant points should be presented either in the introduction or during the summary because the listener remembers more at the beginning and at the ending of speeches. Short and simple words should be used. The words selected should be appropriate to the situation and to the audience.

The vocabulary of the speech should be selected with care. A good vocabulary helps to express common thoughts in an uncommon way. Spoken English should be used instead of written English. Vagueness, jargon, and flowery words should be avoided. Words should be selected that cannot be mistaken in context. Dullness should be avoided by the occasional use of humor and figures of speech. Striking and unusual words add color to a conversation. The use of such techniques as exaggeration, irony, unexpected turns, poking fun at authority, etc., can be used to enlighten the speech. The speech as a whole should be moving. Enthusiasm will capture an audience's interest level.

Practicing the Speech

All speeches should be practiced aloud at least once before giving them to a training class. This is often called a *dry run*. Practice, but do not over do it. A *dry run* is typically conducted before a group of peers. The room is set up in the same way as it will be set up on the day of the presentation. It is very important for the speaker to take this *dry run* seriously. It is hard to take it seriously though. I find it difficult to "act" out my presentation. I tend to skim through the information. If your peers are doing their job, they will insist that you give your entire presentation including distributing handouts and conducting the "question-and-answer" session.

Too much rehearsing can lead to memorizing, which will make your talk too mechanical. Memorized presentations often lack spontaneity and naturalness, because the speaker concentrates on recalling words instead of ideas. It is very annoying and frustrating to the audience when the speaker stumbles through a speech. Words should be spoken clearly and should not be run together. The voice should be projected so it can give force to the message. The speech should be practiced in front of a group of your peers, or if you prefer, practiced in front of a mirror. These practice sessions will help to uncover any problems in the speech or with the visual aids, and to prepare for unexpected complications.

Delivering the Presentation

Handouts

The presentation begins when the procedures analyst walks into the classroom. If handouts are available, they should be held until the end of the training class. They could include a relevant policy or procedure and/or exhibits and charts. The speaker should tell the audience early in the class that handouts will be passed out at the conclusion. If speaker notes have been prepared, these could be handed out to attendees as they come into the room or placed on the tables for them to pick up. It is also a good idea to give a business card, if you have one, to all participants. This gives them the opportunity to call and discuss issues at their own convenience at a later date.

Delivering your Speech

The speaker should begin the class by giving an introduction to the selected subject matter. A good opening can immediately arouse the interest of the audience whereas a poor opening may lose an audience. The purpose, objectives, and length of class should then be stated. The introduction and the purpose should be presented within the first five minutes of the class because the listener tends to remember more at the beginning of a training class. The main thesis should then be presented, with all supporting illustrations. Depending on the type of speech selected, the speaker could introduce visual aids at this time or he could pose a question or a problem to the audience to promote discussions. When the time for the class is nearing its end, the speaker should summarize the main points presented and make any inferences necessary.

Communicating Ideas and Feelings

The speaker should be sincere and natural when delivering the speech. A person who speaks candidly can often gain listeners even if his words do not flow easily. A person who speaks in a smooth and natural way will keep the interest of the audience. Jerkiness in the voice creates uneasiness in the audience.

The self-confident speaker has an erect but comfortable posture. He has easy movements; free of fidgeting and jerkiness; eye-to-eye contact with his listeners; earnestness and energy in his voice, and an alertness of mind that enables him to adapt remarks to the demands of the occasion. Integrity, knowledge, self-confidence, and skill of delivery reflect the characteristics of a good speaker.

Body Movement

Physical activity should be used to reinforce ideas. This also helps to communicate and dissipate one's nervousness and tension. Movement arouses interest. The movement should be natural, easy, and purposeful. It should spring from a genuine desire to communicate. The use of gestures and an erect posture can captivate an audience. The hands should be used as much as possible to illustrate a point. The speaker should avoid leaning on a table, looking out a window, looking at the floor, sitting on a table and swinging his legs, cracking knuckles, folding and unfolding arms, adjusting his clothing, putting both hands behind the back, putting hands into pockets, or clutching the podium.

The speaker should remain close to the audience. The audience needs to feel that the speaker is one of them. The speaker should maintain eye contact at all times. If the speaker has trouble looking at someone in the eye, he could try looking at his forehead. The speaker should make them think he is eager to have them understand or believe the ideas being presented. The speaker does not want the audience to think he is not interested in the subject matter.

The speaker should avoid rambling on or showing off and most of all, he should accept criticism with dignity. If the speaker shows visible irritation to criticism, this puts him at a disadvantage with the listeners and may discredit the entire presentation. If there is much discussion about any issue that is not relevant to the presentation, then the speaker could request that the discussion be taken off-line. The discussion could continue during a break or at the end of the presentation. Arrangements could be made to discuss the issue on another day.

Feedback and Evaluation

The procedures analyst should ask for an evaluation of his training style and the information conveyed through an evaluation form. This information can be very useful for future training classes. It is best if this evaluation is done by the participants before they leave the room. The material is fresh in their minds at this point and they can provide the best evaluation at this time. Otherwise, for those in a hurry, you could permit them to return the evaluation through the mail.

Summary

The procedures analyst has played an important role in researching, writing, distributing, and implementing the policies and procedures system. Once the policies and procedures have been distributed, they are considered carried out. Through training classes, the employees are taught how, when, and where to use guidelines established in the policies or procedures. Left alone, the employees would have to learn these guidelines by trial and error. The trained employee needs less time to carry out assignments and is usually able to achieve job proficiency much sooner than if he had not been properly trained.

The job of training is shared by management and the procedures analyst. Once a policy or procedure is distributed, management personnel should take the time to understand its content so that they can communicate it to their employees. If management does not do an adequate job of disseminating the policy or the procedure, the employee should learn by trial and error. The procedures analyst has a shared responsibility to ensure that the employee understands the content of a policy or procedure.

Chapter 9

Revisions

Revisions to Policies and Procedures

Once policies and procedures are written, approved, distributed, implemented, and trained, it is expected that the content will not change any time soon. However, change is inevitable for a variety of reasons. Some of these reasons may include change in company vision, mission, strategy, core business processes, management, laws, or a procedure that just does not work. Any type of change to the business process could result in a revision. Revisions come in the form of additions, changes, or deletion of text, figures, illustrations, or forms. The entire policy or procedure could be rewritten when the business process undergoes a major change.

The task of revising policies and procedures should not be handled any differently than writing new policies and procedures.

> An established policy or procedure that does not reflect current practices is about as effective as having no written guidelines.

Ensuring that a policy or procedure is kept up-to-date is a major task and should not be treated lightly by either management or by the procedures department. The effectiveness of the procedures analyst could be measured by how well he writes and revises policies and procedures, by how well the policies and procedures are received and used by employees, and by his plans to keep the company manual current.

When reviewing or revising policies and procedures, all of the methods and guidelines included in the first eight chapters should be used to write the necessary revisions. There are only a few differences in technique between writing and revising policies and procedures.

Research Techniques

Review Plan

A plan for keeping policies and procedures current should be set up by management and by the procedures department. A time period should be established when specific policies and procedures are to be tested for current effectiveness. For example, business travel guidelines could be reviewed every six months. Tax procedures could be reviewed once per year before tax season starts. A minimum and a maximum review time should be set for each policy or procedure with 24 months being the maximum for any policy or procedure. Naturally, any policy or procedure should be reviewed if a situation occurs that suggests a change might be in order, e.g., a tax law change or a change in vision or strategy.

Policies and procedures may be reviewed collectively, or individually. When reviewing a policy or procedure, the procedures analyst should apply certain test criteria to decide if the policy or procedure actually needs revising. These criteria include, but are not limited to:

1. Is the policy or procedure written in the current writing format?
2. Is the content comprehensive, up-to-date, and does it cover most contingencies?
3. Are the ideas presented in a logical and easy-to-read format?
4. Do all forms, exhibits, and illustrations reflect the most current information?
5. Are the policy or procedural statements indisputable?
6. Are the control points at strategic places?

If the answer is "no" to any of these questions, then the policy or procedure should be revised.

Occasionally, the procedures analyst will be able to simply change one small section to ensure a policy or procedure conforms to current practices. At other times, the procedures analyst will have to do a thorough analysis of a specific policy or procedure before it can be rewritten. Otherwise, past mistakes may be repeated. The entire process may have changed scope and a new outlook may yield a totally different solution.

Refer to my book, "Achieving 100% Compliance of Policies and

Procedures" for details and an example layout on setting up a review plan. An entire chapter is devoted to this subject.

Sources of Revisions

A common source for revisions, other than from the review plan, is from the user. The major user may submit a recommendation for a revision or may request that a specific policy or procedure be reviewed. The procedures analyst should be careful not to fall into the trap of accepting a proposed change from a single user when there are many users who may want to be involved in changes to the specific policy or procedure. The procedures analyst should keep track of all the users of any particular policy or procedure. When one user wishes to make a change, the other users should be contacted to ensure concurrence.

Form Changes

Typically, any change in a form contained within one or more policies or procedures should require the corresponding policy or procedure to be reviewed. If the form title, the form number, and the function of the form does not change, then the content of the policy or the procedure may not require a revision. The new form could simply be a replacement for the old form. The form instructions may have to be changed because of a revised form. Whenever there is a change, no matter how small, the policy or procedure should be reviewed to ensure the content still conforms to current practices. The addition of a form would necessitate a revision. A definition would be added if one does not already exist for a new form.

When an existing form is revised, a decision should be made concerning the current supply of forms. If the existing supply is usable, the procedures analyst may order the new forms and either put them aside in a temporary location or ask the designated forms stockroom to hold the new forms until the old supply of forms is depleted. If the existing supply of forms is small and/or the change in the form reflects a cost savings, then the procedures analyst may find it necessary to discard all outdated forms once the new form has been received.

Writing, Coordinating, and
Approving the Revised Draft

Following the necessary research for the suggested revision, the procedures analyst can actually write the proposed revision. Decisions need to be made regarding minor (sentence change, a few words changed, a new logo is added to a form, etc.) and major (process is changed, new form added, or responsibility changed, etc.) revisions. For minor revisions, the complete approval process may not be required. It may only require the major user, the procedures analyst, and the final approval authority. For major revisions, the draft revision should go through the same process as for new policies or procedures.

For all revisions, any table of contents (numerical, alphabetical, or keyword) should be updated. The *Revision History* (section 2.0 of the writing format) should be updated with the new revision number and a brief description of the modification. For larger manuals, it can make sense to create a *Revision Table* for the manual itself. The cover page makes a logical place for this revision table.

Distribution of Revised Policies and Procedures

The revision document should be forwarded to all manual holders with a manual revision notice. This way the procedures analyst can explain the changes to the policy or the procedure and explain how to discard the previous version and replace it with this version. This process is very important because users tend to be lazy and file the new revision in front of or behind the old revision. This can cause too many problems if the wrong copy of the policy or procedure is used.

Depending on the alternate methods of distribution selected, this notice of revisions could be published in a bulletin, company newspaper, memorandum, or email message. Refer to Chapter 7 for a discussion of distribution methods.

Implementation of Revised Policies and Procedures

Implementing a revision to a policy or a procedure should be treated the same as implementing a new policy or procedure. When the revised policies or procedures are distributed, the procedures analyst should ensure that the major points changed are highlighted. If the changes are not brought to the attention of the reader, anyone unfamiliar with the policy or procedure may overlook the revisions. The procedures analyst should ensure that the control point (in the case where a person has been selected monitor a certain phase of a procedure), or "watchdog" thoroughly understands the revised policy or procedure before it is distributed to employees. The use of a control point (person, form, or software package) could be highlighted when the policy or procedure is distributed to the manual holders.

If the change can be clearly defined in several sentences or paragraphs when the policy or the procedure is distributed, then a training class may not be necessary. In most cases, however, a training class is a good idea if you want to be fairly certain that the information in the policy or procedure is thoroughly understood. Recall that when a training class is used that you should also make plans to make mentors and coaches available to help those being trained to retain the material.

Revisions to Revisions

The first time the original policy or procedure is revised, it is called *revision 1.0*. This revision is now treated as the original. When revision 1.0 is revised, the new revision is called *revision 1.1*. This second revision is actually a *revision to a revision*. It is common to see many revisions to specific policies or procedures such as those that describe business travel or employee benefits. A revision to a revision is treated the same as for any new policy or procedure.

Summary

The procedures analyst should write revisions to policies and procedures in the same manner as when writing new policies and procedures. Making revisions to established policies and procedures may seem to be a waste of time but, to the contrary, writing revisions is just as important as writing new policies and procedures. Sometimes, it is more important to ensure that an established policy or procedure conforms to current practices than to begin the process of writing a new policy or procedure. With a review plan, specific policies and procedures are reviewed at regular intervals. Suggestions, recommendations, or requirements for changes come from sources such as the user, the parent company, or new state legislation. The procedures analyst should always keep his eyes and ears open to general conversations around the organization. He may be surprised as to the number of different policies and procedures which are alluded to in these casual conversations. When a policy or procedure is revised, any form affected by the revision should also be changed. Similarly, each time a form is changed, the procedures analyst should make the appropriate changes in those policies and procedures in which the form is referenced.

Once the revised policies and procedures have been approved, the documents should be distributed immediately to the current manual holders. If the revision is significant, the procedures analyst should decide if it would be worthwhile to hold a training class. The procedures analyst should highlight the important points of the policy or the procedure when distributing the revision. Often the manual holder will put aside a new or revised policy or procedure until he has the time to read it. If the policy or procedure has been highlighted, the reader is more likely to glance at the front page of the revision changes than to flip through the pages of the policy or the procedure to find the referenced changes.

Chapter 10

ON-LINE MANUALS

On-line Manuals

The term *On-line Manual* is no longer a simple term. A few years ago when manuals were printed and companies were just getting into local area networks (LAN) for sharing electronic information, the on-line manual was not much more than a replica of the printed manual. Using the capabilities of a LAN, it is possible to convert printed manuals directly to a computer screen. In other words, you could convert your printed manuals, word-for-word, for display on a computer monitor. This direct conversion method could be enhanced by hypertext links, help menus, and fast search capabilities provided by the LAN.

The typical on-line policies and procedures manual displays topics one section at a time. Since the *Basic Writing Format* discussed in Chapter 4 consists of seven sections, the conversion to single-topic displays is an easy transition. The same guidelines for writing a printed manual apply to on-line manuals. All of the techniques presented in this book can be used for on-line manuals. The focus of this chapter is on showing the advantages and disadvantages of on-line manuals as well as showing you possible ways to convert your printed documents to electronic display. Studies have concluded that it is easier to read information that is presented one topic at a time. It is your choice as to whether you want to display procedural topics in short chunks of information or to replicate your printed documents on a computer display. You may even find that the display of singular topics is an easier way for users to view and read policies and procedures.

There are many differences between printed and on-line manuals. A few of the more important ones are highlighted below:

1. On-line manuals are electronic and access is quick; printed manuals are often bulky and contain multiple volumes that are difficult to access quickly;

2. On-line manuals can be updated instantly and be distributed companywide simultaneously; printed manuals can take several days, if not weeks, to distribute and they are generally out-of-date before they're distributed;

3. On-line manuals can be resized for easy reading and most keywords can be rapidly searched; printed manuals can be bulky and cumbersome and can be hard to find;

4. On-line manuals cannot be removed from the computer and cannot become "lost"; printed manuals are often lost in the users' environment and carried off by a single user and not returned;

5. On-line manuals can use *clickable* hypertext and help facilities; with printed manuals, references can be made to documents, but they have to be retrieved and searched before the referenced information can be found.

Manual Systems Must Precede the On-line System

While it may seem like creating an on-line policies and procedures system is the proper thing to, it is not the first step in establishing a new policies and procedures system. This is a mistake often made by companies who think that the latest and greatest technology is far superior to manual systems. While this could be true, it will only be true once you have developed a well-documented, working system of printed policies and procedures. It is very difficult to design an on-line manual without having a printed manual system already in place.

It is important to have this measurement tool (printed manual system) in place before spending a large amount of time and money on a new tool. This argument holds true for any new system you might be researching. For example, you wouldn't want to jump into an electronic forms system unless you were working from a successful manual forms system. It is far easier to convert from a fully formed system of forms than to try to figure out the details of an expensive electronic forms system the first time!

Since a policies and procedures system is ongoing, you could start making a conversion to on-line manuals after several years of success with your policies and procedures system. Many of the questions and problems you will have encountered with a printed manual system will probably also be encountered with an on-line manual. With this experience behind you, it will be much easier to make this conversion. Additionally, with the support of your company's computer specialists, the conversion can be carefully planned and then turned over to them for the implementation of the conversion and ongoing maintenance. These computer specialists should become a part of the team working with the conversion process from the printed manuals to an on-line manual.

Dual-Manual System: Printed and On-line

One point that I have not discussed is that you may need both a printed manual and an on-line system of policies and procedures. For example, if your company is large and has many locations, it is possible that some offices may not have the capability to access an on-line manual. This is the case for several large banks in the United States where they have rural offices in small towns. These rural banks do not even have computers. It is not unusual to find companies where employees don't have computers on their individual desks. For them, a printed manual would be useful. And of course, some people dislike using computers. Another less obvious reason for having this dual system is for those few times that the on-line system experiences down time.

Dual-manual systems seem to be commonplace for those companies that use some kind of electronic on-line manual. There are certain circumstances where a printed manual is preferred to electronic manuals. Examples include: orientation manual, benefits overview, and the employee handbook. Employee handbooks are generally distributed during employee orientation. Later, the employee can be directed to a network for updates to the manual. While these employee handbooks are generally passed out in a printed format, they are rarely referred to at a later date because the on-line manual is easier to access and search.

On-line Documentation:
The First Step to Electronic Communication

On-line documentation lacks a single, clear, well-agreed upon definition. Some view it as information displayed on a computer screen. Others view it as a resource that may include help messages, reference guides, and tutorials. Some will rely on prompts and menus to remind them of what information to enter at each point in a program. Users often use computer tutorials and help facilities to learn how to operate a system. Users rely on major databases to find relevant information located not only within the on-line manual system but somewhere within the computer network.

On-line documentation embraces a rich diversity, from one-word messages to non-paper media such as animation, music, voice, and video. It uses the computer chiefly to communicate information, despite the format or subject matter or whether the information exists in other forms as well. In this case, the computer is used as a communication medium, instead of as a number-cruncher or wordprocessor.

On-line documentation systems have two essential parts. The first is electronically stored information. This is usually text, but may also include illustrations, voice, other sounds, animations, and video. The second component is a means of accessing that information. On-line documentation requires a way for users to quickly and conveniently find and display the information they need.

The Lure of On-line Documentation

On-line documentation does not eliminate the need for printed documentation. Many organizations turn to on-line documentation in the hope of eliminating the problems of producing printed documents. This is the lure of on-line documentation. In practice, on-line documentation systems do not replace paper documentation and in some cases, the amount of paper documentation is increased due to ability to print on-line documentation. Printing costs can actually increase as users are able to access more information than before through electronic search capabilities. People like to hold the document in their hand. They like to be able to read documents away from the office. Many people still like the feel of paper. They like to read and file it where they can quickly find it again.

114

On-line documentation takes the content, organization, and format of a document and couples it with access capabilities including menus, database retrieval, context sensitivity, navigation, and full-text search. It then displays the document on a computer screen. It is the search capabilities that piece together what we might call the traditional policies and procedures manual system. With an on-line system, you will never actually see a "set of manuals" in the traditional sense of the word. Information, however, will be easy to find and retrieve. On-line documentation is more likely to be current than printed information because it is quicker to produce.

Benefits of an On-line Manual System

On-line documentation, by integrating information with the computer and electronically distributing and accessing information, gives people up-to-date information when they need it. It provides:

1. FAST DISTRIBUTION AND INFORMATION: On-line documents bypass printing and can be distributed electronically. The on-line manual is a *living* document and continually changes; thus, fast and reliable information is critical to an on-line manual system.
2. IMMEDIATE ACCESS TO NEEDED INFORMATION: On-line documents use the power of the computer to locate and display information. They relieve the user of the chore of getting up, walking to a bookcase (or library), finding the correct procedures manual, returning, finding a spot to place it, opening it up, scanning the index or table or contents for the topic sought, and turning to the appropriate page. With on-line search features, not only can the user find the topic they want quickly, but they can find all the topics that reference specific topics with a click of a button.
3. INTEGRATED INFORMATION AND PRODUCT: Manuals do not get lost and products are complete. Documents are updated and information remains current. The user can be assured that the on-line version of a document is the latest available. Printed documents are difficult to update and it becomes more difficult to assure that all manual holders have the same version.
4. BETTER-SUPPORTED PRODUCTS: The strongest benefit of on-

line documentation is successful communication. Expressing ideas in a timely and reliable manner are some of the expected results of an on-line manual. With computer specialists as a part of the policies and procedures team, support can be rapid and efficient. This improved support can lead to user satisfaction.

Designing an On-line
Policies and Procedures Manual

While it is tempting to convert your printed policies and procedures manual directly to display, content should normally be modified for easy display on a computer monitor. The on-line manual should make reading easy and be user friendly. The same guidelines used for printed company manuals can also be used when designing policies and procedures for an on-line manual system. The more important elements in this chapter are highlighted. These include the involvement of teams, using the manual, making information accessible, organizing the documents, using hypertext, and using on-line help.

Teams for On-line Manuals

Selecting the cross-functional team to support the on-line manual is an easy task. In most cases, the team should consist of the same individuals that participated on the cross-functional team for the printed company manual. Using the same team composition will be beneficial because of their knowledge of the relevant business processes and because they will be able to help with the implementation of the new on-line manual. The team leader is still the procedures analyst. However, the team should be expanded to include computer specialists. The layout, search capabilities, and reference capabilities should become a function of the computer support personnel.

Organizing On-line Documents
Into Short Individual Topics

A major difference between writing printed manuals and writing on-line manuals is that on-line information is often divided into short individual topics for easy display. Procedural information, reference information, statements of purpose, examples, and other self-contained information types support a modular, action-oriented approach. The use of simple and short purpose statements will help users decide whether they have found the right procedure. These statements can be written as standalone topics or placed in context at the beginning of the policy or procedure. If you are concerned that users will find even the simplest purpose statements difficult, you should consider putting a link to a layered, standalone statement. Users can then access the information when they are in doubt about the purpose of the steps.

On-line documentation systems, and computers in general, work best with discrete chunks of information, such as numbers, characters, words, phrases, paragraphs, and passages. Topics should be designed for convenient display and easy retrieval. The easier it is to find information, the more often the system will be used. This results in better communication.

The on-line manual should be set up similar to your printed manual in that it will have tables of contents (numerical, alphabetical, and keyword) that reference and link to specific policies and procedures. Each section of the *Basic Writing Format* will be included. The only difference is that each of the seven sections will be displayed on its own set of pages. The topics can be linked through hypertext jumps. Users have the option of reading them in any order, and topics need no formal transitional language to link them together. Each on-line topic is presumed to stand alone. Refer to Appendices I and J for samples of two sections from a printed policy that were converted to individual pages. If this method of conversion is not acceptable to your company, you can always revert to one-for-one conversion of your printed manuals. I would recommend that you experiment with different formats and displays for the on-line policies and procedures manual.

Pop-up definitions can be used with on-line manuals. These definitions allow you to define all the terms on a screen. They can be accessed through hypertext jumps. Information topics could describe typical scenarios that users might follow to achieve a goal. Scenarios are detailed, realistic examples of how users might use a particular procedure or series of procedures to accomplish a complicated task. Scenarios help users understand and act upon complicated instructions.

Easily understood examples could also be used. As in printed documentation, examples are a good way to communicate ideas effectively and to clarify difficult ideas. A layered hypertext-supported design allows you to include even lengthy examples without affecting the brevity of a procedure or the simplicity of a conceptual overview. If you include a button or labeled link to an example of a procedure or idea, the user has the choice of accessing the link.

The best planned structures become irrelevant without well-structured information behind them. Besides outlining the general structure of information, your content specification should establish the structure of individual topics. For example, you might decide that each topic will describe a procedure and that all procedures will start with an explanation of when the procedure should be completed, followed by steps for completing the procedure. You might further decide that each step will provide feedback that allows the user to verify that the step has been completed correctly. When you specify the detailed structure for each type of information topic you plan, then the topics created will be consistent and the structure and content predictable. Users will know what to expect once they reach the topic of their choice.

If these discrete chunks of data are not organized in this manner, it will make it more difficult for computer support personnel and the procedures analyst to determine a suitable electronic format that would be easily accessible. The document should be organized in a way that meets user expectations and in a way that can be the most usable by computer support personnel. Users should consult the computer support personnel in advance of submitting the data for conversion to electronic information.

Displaying the Information

Visual design of on-line documentation involves the traditional items of page layout, such as typography, white space, line length, margins, and so forth. In addition, it may concern new choices for the designer like the use of color, blinking, and reverse video. The on-line documents should look like printed documents and allow the same methods of access. Care needs to be taken not to compromise readability and display problems. For example, the on-line display could be smaller than the printed page and it could be shaped differently. The document should be displayed in a way that reduces the disruption to the user's work. If possible, the document should be displayed in a small fixed message area or as an independent window the user can position and size on the screen. There are many possibilities for correct display and easy readability. I have several sources of on-line documentation books in the bibliography.

Making Information Accessible

The method for locating information is different in online documents than printed manuals. Making information accessible requires careful planning and designing of access methods. No system can do this on its own. The way information is accessed should be carefully planned early in the project.

If a topic is difficult to access, fewer people will use the system. The on-line manual system should shorten and simplify the path to the topic of interest. Various ways of accessing information need to be incorporated. These could include the ability to:

1. Find a list of processes, policies, and procedures in a manual that contain similar key words;
2. Browse a single document and print it;
3. Select from menus;
4. Select from directories such as alphabetical indexes, tables of contents, lists of tables, lists of figures; and
5. Retrieve specific topics based on a variety of characteristics.

All possible strategies should be available to the user. It may be beneficial to survey the users to decide how they prefer to access information on both a printed and an on-line system. The goal of an on-line manual is to provide quick access to almost any query. Without quick access, the user may go to another source, possibly a much less reliable one such as a fellow employee who may not be aware of the latest policy or procedure.

Help Facilities

Help information is a new feature to a policies and procedures manual. This is a feature not found in printed manuals. With on-line manuals and the use of layered links, it is now possible to add *clickable* help facilities to the documents. Help information is information delivered to a user, at the user's request, in the context of the user's on-line task. The goal of a help system is not to teach users about the system but to help the user with information about a particular component of the system. Thus, your help system should be designed to aid the user with small, yet specific actions. An effective help system adds to the perceived quality of interactive systems.

The procedure should contain as many help topics as possible and as many layered links as feasible, to help guide the user through a procedural topic. Care should be taken to avoid giving the users too much information or information that they could see as irrelevant. Explanations of the importance of pursuing a course of action (or statements of the consequences of not doing so) may help users understand why the procedures should be performed as indicated. When users understand the potential consequences of a policy or procedure, they are more likely to follow the guidelines therein.

Using Hypertext

Hypertext is a network of interlinked topics, typically browsed by navigating links, viewed in windows, and stored in a database. The essential feature of hypertext is the computer-provided ability to rapidly and automatically follow links within and among documents. One can find information using several strategies. Users can navigate the hypertext, skipping from topic to topic by selecting links. Each topic may display icons or text labels that the user selects to display additional topics.

Furthermore, the wrong links add even more confusion. It is important to understand why you might add links to your on-line system. Hypertext links acknowledge the reading habits of the users while attempting to guide them through on-line information that lacks the signposts that they have always relied on in printed manuals. Links can be used to:

1. Point to other sections of the *Basic Writing Format*, definitions, help menus, and other policies and procedures;
2. Control topic size and appearance;

3. Display graphics; and
4. Call other support.

Hypertext is an important addition to the on-line policies and procedures manual. When policies and procedures are written, links can be established that help the users navigate among the various sections of a document and within all documents on the network. I would suggest using hypertext in layered links to help the user navigate through the policies and procedures on-line manual.

Clear Writing is Essential

When it comes to clear, simple writing, on-line documentation is just like writing printed documentation, only more so. Without clear writing, on-line documents fail. The procedures analyst needs to pay particular attention to the two writing styles. The printed and on-line manuals should contain identical content. The way they will be displayed should be different. This difference needs to be carefully monitored when writing policies and procedures for on-line manuals. Some on-line basics to consider include:

1. Use short, simple, familiar words;
2. Avoid abstract words, computer terminology, contractions, and abbreviations. Use only standard, easily read symbols. If these terms are needed, provide links to definitions;
3. Standardize terms, grammatical patterns, abbreviations, spelling, and special conventions used throughout the system;
4. Avoid or take special care with small words and punctuation marks that are easily overlooked or misread on the computer screen;
5. Write simple sentences and express ideas precisely;
6. Apply a consistent style throughout;
7. Say more with fewer words in less space; in each topic, express just one main idea. Eliminate unnecessary information and electronically cross-reference related topics;
8. Eliminate unnecessary material, keep paragraphs short, and avoid blind references; and
9. Write topics so they can be read in any order. Clearly signal

transitions between topics and provide summaries at points where the user is likely to stop reading.

Converting to an on-line manual does not have to be as complicated as it seems. If you work closely with the computer support personnel on your cross-functional team, then the conversion process will go much easier. You can go slowly and work toward a new writing style for on-line manuals. Keep the points of this chapter in mind when making the conversion. I have included several excellent books on on-line documentation in the bibliography.

Converting Printed Manuals

If you have followed my advice and did not pursue an on-line manual system without first developing a printed manual system that works, then you are ready to convert your printed manual system to an on-line manual. It becomes a matter of rewriting approved policies and procedures. There are two methods of conversion. Either way is acceptable. It just depends on your management's direction for electronic manuals.

First, conversion could be as simple as transferring the printed company manual directly to the company's LAN. With this method, there is not much to rewrite. Search and hypertext capabilities could be added to make it easer to find topics and use help. Actually, this conversion method could be deployed in parallel while your new on-line manual system is being developed.

Second, the printed manual could be rewritten so that each section within each policy or procedure can be reduced to one or two pages. Each document could be rewritten to fit this simplified, single-topic format. One alternative is to extract the information from each section without any changes. The reasons that you might consider rewriting the sections is for better viewing on the computer. There would be a brief summary of the contents of each page along with the information contained within a specific section. Refer to Appendices I and J for two samples of single-topic displays.

Summary

With the rapid movement toward computers, I think it is inevitable that your manual system will be converted to some kind of electronic display. It may mean hiring computer support personnel to work within the policies and procedures department. The question that I am sure still looms in many of your heads, is whether all documents will go on-line sometime in the future? I think this answer is "Yes," but not for at least another 20 years. While the future is taking us closer and closer to total automation, paper is here to stay. You will see more information being made available to you on the computer, but there will still be a need for paper documents. Some people will never give up paper.

In the final chapter of the book, I will explore the use of an Intranet or Extranet for displaying policies and procedures. The similarities to on-line manuals are so close that the difference is becoming more and more fuzzy. Ultimately, I believe that the difference between the two systems becomes a matter of presentation preference.

Chapter 11

Internet and Intranets/Extranets

Internet

The *Internet* provides an easy point-and-click way to find information on hundreds of thousands of computers worldwide using *browser* software. Any platform or operating system can used. The Internet is a collection of websites. The web displays information on your computer screens, such as pages of text and pictures, and can include sound and moving images. Businesses can also use the web to collect information with electronic forms. The importance of the Internet is that it is a *hypertext* information system. This means that instead of reading text in a rigid, linear structure, you can easily skip from one point to another, get more information, go back, jump to other topics, and navigate through the text based on what interests you at the time.

The Internet is fun. An Intranet helps your employees do better jobs. An Extranet helps your company do a better job. The Intranet is an "internal Internet" with a *firewall* that keeps intruders out; an Extranet is an "Intranet with outside access capabilities."

Intranet

An Intranet is "a heterogenous computing environment that promotes the exchange of information." This information exchange occurs among different hardware platforms, but more importantly, the exchange is between different operating system environments. With an Intranet, you have access to all the information, applications, data, knowledge, processes, etc., available in the same window, or the same browser. The Intranet is a private network with Internet technology used as the underlying architecture. The Intranet can link together all of the information in your organization. Intranets enable companies to conduct business better, to keep in better touch with customers; to sell goods and services more effectively; to better integrate all the resources of a corporation, and to help employees work better.

Templates and electronic forms are easy to create on the Intranet. With a sophisticated web searching tool, you need not sift through long pages of information to get what you want. There is no conversion to different formats while waiting for programmers to code all the new systems together, or teams of consultants to sift through your processes.

The "pure" Intranet applies standard Internet technology (protocols and software) on private networks isolated from the public Internet. Most real Intranets include links to the public Internet, using security firewalls to prevent intrusion by outsiders. The Intranet can dramatically lower costs by avoiding paper copies, printing and distribution expenses. It results in increased productivity, because employees are not spending their time looking for information or buried in paper.

Intranets have become an essential corporate information distribution and database tool. Until recently, only large corporations had been able to take advantage of available technologies to develop and maintain Inranets. Intranets, when properly designed, enable cost savings through the centralization of services on servers. Another cost savings benefit arises from lower employee training costs.

The introduction of new, easy-to-use Intranet tools makes this powerful technology accessible to any size organization. It applies the advantages of Internet to reach and distribute information within your organization. Intranets span continents, link global companies together seamlessly with the information needed to compete in this ever-evolving, knowledge-based economy. The convenience of the Intranet permits you to use your existing computer network and still incorporate data from the outside world. The Intranet is the WAN/LAN, client/server, PC, or UNIX computer that you have been using all along in your organization to do your work.

The problem has been that the machines, software, and communication systems have been proprietary. You could not have internal communication of all data and information without a team of programmers and new software for every new piece of information.

126

The prime difference between establishing policies and procedures on the LAN (on-line manuals) and referencing them on an Intranet is that with on-line manuals you are limited to basic text, flat graphical files, and specific computers and peripherals hooked together to a network server. This costs money and there are issues of compatibility, maintenance, and costs. The web is already in place, any computer can be used, and the cost of a browser and server is not much more than a telephone bill.

When information can be pulled instantly, decision makers are able to analyze business processes, business opportunities, and business goals much faster. It follows that more employees can become decision makers. Projects are managed more efficiently. Customer requirements are documented and followed. Development occurs in a shared electronic development space rather than between meetings, telephone calls, and individual schedules. The Intranet is cheaper to print, faster to distribute, easier to update, and can present a uniform face to your employees.

The Intranet integrates corporate communications, departmental communications, group communications, and individual communications into a place that provides up-to-date, quality, and instant information to anyone in the organization whenever and wherever needed. Hundreds of documents, presentations, notes, software, policies, procedures, and training materials can be stored on-line. These resources are available to everyone 24 hours a day.

The Intranet can also solve some of your ISO 9000 requirements. First, you can provide all information on-line in a single location. Secondly, you can identify processes, metrics, and project contacts on-line. Since everyone can access the Intranet, it becomes a solid singular source, or repository, that satisfies many ISO requirements.

An Intranet web can help you automate business processes. For example, many organizations are using Intranet web sites to automate the distribution and administration of internal documents, including policies and procedures, benefit selections, retirement information, important human resources information, telephone lists, and job postings. Electronic distribution eliminates the high cost of updating and distributing paper documents every time an update occurs.

Your company can use an Intranet to produce, distribute, and reach its own communications inside your company, using the same tools people use to produce, distribute, and reach information on the Internet outside. This means by using a web browser, email, file transfers, and newsgroups, employees in your company can reach company news, employee phone books, human resources information, product specifications, pricing information, software, data, and of course, policies and procedures. Intranets can be especially useful to those employees who telecommute. With email and other Internet tools, anything you can do on the computer at your desk, you can do on the road. Laptop computers have become commonplace for employees as they can access a computer network from almost anywhere in the world. Laptops can be used at the beach, on an airplane, in a hotel room, on a bus, on a train, or in an automobile. Telephones that act as modems mean that you can information almost anywhere, any time you feed to locate and retrieve data.

Extranet

An *Extranet* is a network of Intranets coupled with Internet capabilities. It is typically behind a security firewall, just as an Intranet usually is, and closed to the public, but is open to selected partners. An Extranet is not confined to the sponsoring organization like the Intranet. It can reach outside the organization, particularly to the suppliers and customers with whom the organization wants to take an active role. With an Extranet, you can share information such as the publishing of the latest product information, price lists, press releases, and even on-line demonstrations. Project teams can be built that extend beyond single organizations to customer and vendor locations. In these different firms, the differences in equipment and location will be even greater. This is especially true for Electronic Commerce or Electronic Data Interchange (EDI) applications where business partners may want access to the company's processes and procedures to supplement their understanding and use of electronic commerce or EDI applications.

Your business partners can place orders and process payments electronically. A good example of this is the Federal Express do-ityourself shipment tracking system. Customers can track their own shipments without requiring intervention by FedEx employees.

The Extranet is especially useful to employees who travel. Special forms for such functions as timekeeping or expense reports can be made accessible. Employees, using their laptop computers and modems from anywhere in the world can fill in their weekly time sheets or submit current expenses. The Extranet could even provide feedback as to the accuracy of input and the processing steps. The way policies and procedures are written and viewed could be completely different in the Extranet world.

While I can envision several instances where vendors or suppliers may need access to specific policies and procedures for electronic commerce reasons, I believe that the use of a company's policies and procedures manual from the outside world would be limited. This subject of Extranets has been mentioned as a courtesy for readers to think about, but it is not the subject of this chapter or book. If interested, I would recommend searching the library indexes for books on the subject.

Linking Policies and Procedures
to the Company's Intranet

With the versatility of the Intranet, it is an excellent place to reference policies and procedures. They can be integrated into the other uses of an Intranet for your company including such items as company news, employee phone books, human resources information, product specifications, pricing information, cafeteria menus, or any kind of documents or data your management wants to provide.

With the Intranet, the distribution of policies and procedures is a snap. Instead of distributing policies or procedures every time a change is made, the policy or procedure can be emailed to every user and "living" locations can be identified for easy reference. No longer does the employee have to worry about filing every policy or procedure or be concerned if he has the most current version when referencing or applying the information. Training is also quick and easy and it saves on travel time, meeting preparations, and numerous telephone calls to explain and interpret changes.

The Policies and Procedures Department should be the only group allowed to access the policies and procedures section of the Intranet. This control ensures that policies and procedures are coordinated just like the printed company manual. The procedures analyst will work with his cross-functional team and develop a draft policy or procedure. It will be the procedures analyst who obtains the necessary approvals and uploads the information to the Intranet. No one else should be allowed this access as it could compromise the integrity of the policies and procedures themselves. Actually, this type of manual helps to solve one of the many problems procedures analyst face, that is, how to ensure that only properly approved policies and procedures are distributed to employees. For example, I have seen several examples where an employee will write a procedure and distribute it without going through the normal approval channels. With the Intranet, the procedures analyst could set special "read-only" rights to those reading the policies and procedures. Only the Policies and Procedures Department would have "write" privileges.

I might add that if this function is given to a department that updates the Intranet (such as Information Services) rather than the procedures analyst, the corporate policies and procedures manual might not stay current as policies and procedures typically take a lower priority to other departments. The procedures analyst should be the only one who can make changes to policies and procedures. There should be no exception to this rule.

It is not the purpose of this book to explore the mechanics or the software applications used to create this Intranet other than to say that there are many easy-to-use software packages on the market for designing Intranets. There are also many books at the local library or bookstore on this subject. I have included several excellent resources in the bibliography including a "Hands-On Intranet" guidebook.

Standards of the Intranet

As with any communication system that involves the transfer and communication of company information, a policy for the Intranet needs to be established before the Intranet is made available to all employees. Like policies and procedures, the format should be consistent from screen to screen. A standard infrastructure and operating environment allows integration of applications with the Intranet in order to really maximize its potential to facilitate business communication and application. Intranet design can become rampant if it goes uncontrolled. Some of these standards include style guides, security guidelines, answers to frequently asked questions, resource creation and control (such as policies and procedures) software use, Internet access, navigational tools, and search capabilities.

Documents Should be Kept Current

While the Intranet is an excellent tool for referencing policies and procedures and related information, it is not without problems. Once a policy or procedure is created for the Intranet, the procedures analyst needs to ensure that this "Intranet" document stays accurate and current. He also needs to ensure that links are not "broken." If information is not current, then it will not be used and employees are apt to look for alternate sources. These are just some of the pitfalls that the procedures analyst should continue to monitor. If employees resist your new web pages and tend to prefer printed manuals, then the problem probably lies with your presentation on the Intranet and how easy the information is to reach.

Converting Printed Manuals for
Use on an Intranet

The conversion of a printed manual to a system of policies and procedures on the Intranet is very similar to the on-line manual except for its presentation on the screen. The methods used to create the initial policies and procedures, or any revisions, follow the same guidelines as when creating new policies and procedures. With the Intranet manual, there are many features that can be added to assist the user in viewing and understanding policies and procedures. For example, the use of hypertext links can be most helpful when the definitions section references outside governmental agencies, regulations, or other pertinent information. If a policy discusses the requirements of a governmental agency, it becomes an easy task to create a link to that governmental agency within the procedural message. If ISO 9000 Standards are being addressed, links can be created to the most current guidelines on these standards and also to the other companies that have been ISO 9000 certified. An on-line claim form could be linked to a health carrier for easy processing. The possibilities are enormous and I am excited about the prospects that the Intranet brings. It helps to create a *living* policies and procedures manual.

I have created a sample of a possible way to convert a printed procedure to an Intranet format; refer to Appendix K. Using a Microsoft term, "Shared Borders," I have created a consistent format with repeatable top, side, and bottom borders. The top border is used for the title of the policy or procedure, the number, and the effective date of the policy or procedure. The bottom border is for the table of contents and glossary. The side bar is used for the navigational tools for the web site. In this case, I have included the seven headings of the *Basic Writing Format* as discussed in Chapter 4. By clicking on any *underscored text*, it sends a message to the computer to find that referenced item and display it in the middle of the screen, or to the right of the navigational bar.

While not shown, the phrase, "policies and procedures" could be added to the navigational bar on the company's Intranet. A link could be set up whereby one click will open a "Master Table of Contents" for all policies and procedures. This table of contents would enable the user to scroll down a list of policies and procedures and click on the selected document. A search feature could also be added so that any keyword could be entered. The result would be a list of policies and procedures that contain that keyword. A single click on any of the "found" policies and procedures would retrieve that document. The use of the "back" or "forward" button on the browser software would enable the user to navigate through the policies and procedures.

The procedures analyst should plan to work closely with the computer specialists assigned to his team to understand and develop documentation for the Intranet. I would also recommend that the procedures analyst read about Intranets and Extranets so he can provide solid information to those that will be using the Intranet policies and procedures manual. The procedures analyst needs to continually improve his knowledge about current and future technology.

Summary

An Intranet can be home-grown but care should be taken with the Extranet as information can get to the outside world. With the current technology, the Internet is becoming more and more popular and using an Intranet for company resources is becoming commonplace. Companies still use on-line manuals on a LAN but they are becoming less and less popular. The question will become one of cost. Intranets have often been viewed as very expensive; but with recent technology, the cost is approaching that of an on-line manual in a company's LAN. There are inherent advantages for a policies and procedures system to be connected to the Internet.

The sharing of information was an important development for both the Intranet and the Extranet, because until recently, the typical personal computer (PC) was an individual-use tool with a suite of desktop applications intended for individual use. Some application suites are now developing workgroup capability, but at the heart, these are still single-user applications.

Fundamentally, none of these tools have been designed to share information easily across an enterprise. Word processors were designed to create printed documents, sharing them with others was an afterthought. Even in the typical network installation, file servers were designed to provide shared access to files and applications, but not for easy searching or retrieval. Web technology has made it easier for users to navigate through massive amounts of information. This is why the Intranet and Extranet are such important developments. The procedures analyst should make use of as many tools as possible.

Afterword

I wrote *Establishing a System of Policies and Procedures* out of a sincere desire to help procedures analysts write successful policies and procedures manuals in three formats: printed, on-line, and Intranet/Extranet webs. When I first wrote *Business Policies and Procedures Handbook* in the early 1980's, I had written everything I knew about producing a successful printed manual. I have shared my successes with you, which I might add, represent the best of my twenty-five years of experience. Growth is a never-ending process. As your knowledge deepens about company visions, missions, strategies, and business processes, so will your ability to develop the important *art of writing successful policies and procedures*. I have included my address and email at the front of this book. Please tell me what you like and send me suggestions for improvement. Let me know what perplexes you.

Although I cannot guarantee success, the principles offered in this book have been successful for me in several multinational companies and by hundreds of others who have sent me nice "thank you" notes for my first book on policies and procedures. The principles in this book work for those who use them.

Use this book as a primer to my other three books on policies and procedures. Each book is different and will add to your experience of creating a successful system of policies and procedures. My books are best read in the following sequence:

1. "7 Steps to Better Written Policies and Procedures"
2. "Best Practices in Policies and Procedures"
3. "Achieving 100% Compliance of Policies and Procedures'

Bibliography/ Recommended Reading

Baker, Richard H. *Extranets: The Complete Sourcebook.* New York, New York: McGraw-Hall, 1997.

Barnett, Robert. *Practical Playscript.* Canberra, Australia: Robert Barnett & Associates, 1993.

Barnett, Robert. *Managing Business Forms.* Canberra, Australia: Communication Research Institute of Australia, Incorporated, 1988.

Burleson, Clyde W. *Effective Meetings, The Complete Guide.* New York, NY: John Wiley & Sons, Inc., 1990.

Carnegie Mellon University, Software Engineering Institute. *The Capability Maturity Model: Guidelines for Improving the Software Process.* Reading, Massachusetts: Addison-Wesley, 1994.

Dasan, Vasanthan S. and **Ordorica, Luis R.** *Hands-On Intranets.* Mountain View, California: Sun Microsystems Press, 1998.

Davenport, Thomas H. *Process Innovation.* Boston, Massachusetts: Harvard Business School Press, 1993.

Derrick, Dan. *Network Know-How: Concepts, Cards & Cables.* New York, NY: Osborne McGraw-Hill, 1992.

Emery, Vince. *How to Grow Your Business on the Internet.* Scottsdale, Arizona: Coriolis Group, Inc., 1996.

Fox, William M. *Effective Group Problem Solving.* San Francisco, CA: Jossey-Bass Publishers, 1988.

Gralla, Preston. *How Intranets Work*. Emeryville, California: Ziff-Davis Press, 1996.

Green, Marj and **Jarvis, Brian M.** and **McGarry, Dennis J.** and **Gerhard, Rick A.** *The Business Forms Handbook*. Alexandria, Virginia: National Business Forms Association, 1990.

Hackos, Joann T. and **Stevens, Dawn M.** *Standards for Online Communication*. New York, NY: John Wiley & Sons, Inc., 1997.

Hammer, Michael and **Champy, James**. *Reengineering the Corporation*. New York, NY: HarperBusiness, 1993.

Hopper, Vincent and **Foote, Ronald**. *Essentials of English*. New York, NY: Barron's Educational Series, Inc., 1990.

Horton, William K. *Designing & Writing Online Documentation*. New York NY: John Wiley & Sons, Inc., 1990.

Hoyle, David. *ISO 9000 Quality Systems Handbook*. UK:Butterworth-Heinemann, 1994.

Lindberg, Roy A. and **Cohn, Theodore**. *Operations Auditing*. New York, NY: AMACOM, 1972.

Moody, Paul. *Decision Making*. New York, NY: McGraw-Hill Book Company, 1983.

Page, Stephen B. *7 Steps to Better Written Policies and Procedures*. Process Improvement Publishing, 2001

Page, Stephen B. *Achieving 100% Compliance of Policies and Procedures*. Process Improvement Publishing, 2000.

Page, Stephen B. *Best Practices in Policies and Procedures*. Process Improvement Publishing, 2002

Page, Stephen B. *Business Policies and Procedures Handbook.* Englewood Cliffs, New Jersey: Prentice-Hall, Inc., 1984.

Pike, Robert W. *Creative Training Techniques Handbook.* Minneapolis, MN: Lakewood Books, 1989.

Resnick, Rosalind and **Taylor, Dave**. *Internet Business Guide.* Indianapolis, IN: Sams.net Publishing, 1995.

Roberts, Lon. *Process Reengineering.* Milwaukee, Wisconsin: ASQC Quality Press, 1994.

Ross, Tom & Marilyn. *The Complete Guide to Self-Publishing.* Cincinnati, Ohio: Writer's Digest Books, 1994.

Sandy, William. *Forging the Productivity Partnership.* New York, NY: McGraw-Hill Publishing Company, 1990.

Spendolini, Michael J. *The Benchmarking Book.* New York, NY: AMACOM, 1992.

Tregoe, Benjamin B. and **Zimmerman, John W.** and **Smith, Ronald A.** and **Tobia, Peter**. *Vision in Action.* New York, NY: A Firestone Book, 1990.

APPENDICES

	Description of Appendix	Chapters
A	Core Business Processes	2
B	Sample Content for Policies and Procedures	2
C	Sample Playscript Procedure	4
D	Sample Policy with Indented Numbering	4
E	Sample Policy without Indented Numbering	4
F	Sample Numerical Table of Contents	7
G	Sample Alphabetical Table of Contents	7
H	Sample Policy with Revision History	4, 9
I	Sample On-line Policy Section	4, 10
J	Sample On-line Responsibilities Section	4, 10
K	Sample Intranet Policy/Procedure Template	11

Company A	Company B	Company C
Market information capture	Customer engagement	Direct business
Market selection	Inventory management and logistics	Plan business
Development of hardware	Product design and engineering	Develop processes
Development of software	Product maintenance	Manage process operation
Development of services	Technology management	Provide personnel support
Production	Production and operations management	Market products and services
Customer fulfillment	Market management	Provide customer service
Customer relationship	Supplier management	Manage products and services
Service	Information management	Provide consultancy services
Customer feedback	Business management	Plan the network
Marketing	Human resource management	Operate the network
Solution integration	Leased and capital asset management	Provide support services
Financial analysis	Legal	Manage information resource
Plan integration		Manage finance
Accounting		Provide technical R&D
Human resources		

Human Resources	Purchasing Department	Sales Management
Employment	Notification	Sales Management
Interviews/Tests	Requisitions	Developing Product
Job Offers	Bill of Materials	Market Analysis
Placement	Ordering	Distribution
Transfers	Inquiries	Supermarkets
Promotions	Quotations	Shopping Centers
Termination	Purchase Order	Chain Stores
Exit Interviews	Subcontracting	Telephone Sales
Severance Pay	Petty Cash	Franchising
Compensation	COD Orders	Trade Practices
Training/Education	Shipping	Pricing
Tuition Assistance	Post-Ordering	Terms of Sale
Safety	Receiving	Discounts
Welfare	Inspection	Premiums
Employee Relations	Invoicing	Sales Organization
Benefits	Purchase Records	Sales Force

Accounting & Finance	Manufacturing Department	Forms Management
Balance Sheet	Bills of Material	Forms Control
Income Statement	NAFTA Guidelines	Form Requisition
Accounting Cycle	Tooling Methods	Forms Analysis
Working Capital	Standard Engineering	Forms Design
Funds Statement	Pick List	Forms Numbering
Inventories	Inventory Control	Form Review
Fixed Assets	Stock Requisitions	Form Approval
Long-Term Debt	Material Transfer	Stock Control
Cost Standards	Master Schedule	Forms Inventory
Tax Standards	Assembly Process	Forms Standards
	On-line Inspection	Forms Buying
	Final Inspection	

Purchase Requisition
No. 100 7/1/1998

Requester	1. Completes Requisition No. 1729, Rev. 8/1/95 with details of request. 2. Obtains charge number from Accounting. 3. Obtains approval from his immediate supervisor. 4. Mails requisition to Purchasing. 5. Keeps second copy for his records.
Purchasing Assistant	6. Sorts mail and routes requisition to appropriate buyer.
Buyer	7. Obtains three bids for items requested. 8. Selects best bid based on purchasing guidelines for selecting vendor. 9. Generates Purchase Order and mails it to selected vendor.

Electronic Mail	No. 100
	Date: 4/1/1998
	Rev. 1.0
	Page 1 of 2

1.0   <u>Purpose</u>

This policy establishes guidelines by which electronic mail, voice systems, and other network mail systems are used at the XYZ Company.

2.0   <u>Revision History</u>

4/1/1998	1.0	New Document

3.0   <u>Persons Affected</u>

All employees.

4.0   <u>Policy</u>

The policy of the XYZ Co. is to inform employees that:

4.1   Electronic mail, voice mail, or network mail systems are company resources and are . . . Etc.

5.0   <u>Definitions</u>

5.1   <u>Electronic Mail (Email)</u> - A group of users that communicate electronically to others users.

Note: Second page not shown.

	No. 100
Electronic Mail	Date: 4/1/1998
	Rev. 1.0
	Page 1 of 2

1.0   Purpose

This policy establishes guidelines by which electronic mail, voice systems, and other network mail systems are used at XYZ Co.

2.0   Revision History

4/1/1998	1.0	New Document

3.0   Persons Affected

All employees.

4.0   Policy

The policy of the XYZ Co. is to inform employees that:

4.1   Electronic mail, voice mail, or network mail systems are company resources and . . . etc.

5.0   Definitions

5.1   Electronic Mail (Email) - A group of users that communicate electronically to others users on the same mail system. . . . . . Etc.

Note: Second page not shown.

144

Numerical Table of Contents

Number	Subject	Dated
	Personnel Relations	
100	Affirmative Action Program	01/05/82
101	(Pre-Assigned)	
102	Personnel Appraisals	05/04/83
103	Wages and Salaries	06/01/83
104	Employee Overtime	08/01/83
Etc . . .		
	Administrative Services	
200	Business Expenses	06/02/82
201	Leased Vehicles	06/18/82
202	Forms Management	05/01/93
203	Material Data Safety Sheets	09/10/94
204	Employee Bulletin Boards	10/01/96
Etc . . .		

Alphabetical Table of Contents

Subject   Number

E

Emergency Evacuation   748
Employee Overtime   104
Employee Separations   121
Etc . . .

F

Family Death   146
Foreign Travel   251
Forms Management   267
Etc . . .

G

Garnishments   147
Grievance Guidelines   150
Etc . . .

	No. 100
Electronic Mail	Date: 7/1/1998
	Rev. 1.1
	Page 1 of 2

1.0 Purpose

This policy establishes guidelines by which electronic mail, voice systems, and other network mail systems are used at the XYZ Company.

2.0 Revision History

4/1/1998	1.0	New Document
7/1/1998	1.1	Added New Form

3.0 Persons Affected

All employees.

4.0 Policy

The policy of the XYZ Co. is to inform employees that:

4.1   Electronic mail, voice mail, or network mail systems are company resources and . . . Etc.

5.0 Definitions

5.1   Electronic Mail (Email) - A group of users that communicate electronically to others users on the same mail system . . . Etc.

Sample On-line POLICY STATEMENT
for a Total Quality Management (TQM) Policy

TQM Policy Statement
No. 1000, Rev. 1.0, 4/1/1998

The policy of the XYZ Company is to:

1.0 Continuously pursue the highest quality in our products and services for exceeding our customers' needs and expectations indefinitely.

2.0 Pursue TQM as a business strategy.

3.0 Continuously improve processes, products, services, and operations so that XYZ Company can constantly offer customers superior value.

4.0 Develop quality improvement objectives and metrics for display companywide, and in departments and work areas.

5.0 Reward groups or individuals for contributions to TQM.

6.0 Evaluate employee contributions to continuous quality improvement appraisal process as part of performance.

7.0 Encourage and promote participation of every XYZ employee in continuous process improvement.

8.0 Train XYZ employees in TQM tools, techniques, and applications for use on the job.

Sample On-line RESPONSIBILITIES SECTION
for a Total Quality Management (TQM) Policy

TQM Responsibilities Section **No. 1000, Rev. 1.0, 4/1/1998**

1.0 The President of the XYZ Company and the TQM Council is responsible for ensuring compliance to this policy.

2.0 The Vice President of TQM is responsible for embedding TQM into the company for ensuring quality improvement is included in strategic plans as a routine way of doing business.

3.0 Department Executives are responsible for pursuing TQM as a fundamental responsibility and for carrying out a continuous improvement plan, including metrics, for all processes under their ownership.

4.0 Managers and supervisors are responsible for creating a supportive environment that requires communications with employees on continuous improvement that leads to submission of suggestions from employees, for improvement and total customer satisfaction.

5.0 Employees are responsible for modeling and fostering TQM and by seeking potential areas of continuous and self development improvement to ensure total customer satisfaction.

6.0 Department TQM Facilitators are responsible for supporting the Department Executive in improving the owned-business processes and for fostering TQM in the Department.

No.   **TITLE**   Date

Navigational Bar	*Shared Border*

Purpose
Revision History
Affected Areas
Policy
Definitions
Responsibilities
Procedures

Related
Procedures

Search of
Keywords

When clicking on *underscored* words, it invokes the hypertext and places the information into this section of the document. When finished reading, you can click on another navigational title. For ease of navigating, you could include *next page* and *previous page* buttons at the bottom of this message.

Example: Click on *Purpose* hypertext for the Electronic Mail Policy and the following pops into this whole area:

Information
Author
Revisions

MASTER
Table of
Contents

PURPOSE

This policy establishes guidelines by which electronic mail, voice systems, and other network mail systems are used at XYZ Co.

Previous Page   Next Page

Numerical Contents   Alphabetical Contents   Glossary